JUST

A crusade for credit by Radiohead's first true fan

Paul McCarthy

© Paul McCarthy, 2024

All rights reserved, including the right to reproduce this book or portions thereof in any form whatsoever, without the prior written permission of the author. While Amsterdam Academy Press and author have used their best efforts in preparing this book, they make no representations or warranties with respect to the accuracy or completeness of the contents of this book and specifically disclaim any implied warranties of merchantability or fitness for a particular purpose. Neither Amsterdam Academy Press nor the author shall be liable for any loss of profit or any other commercial damages, including but not limited to special, incidental, consequential, personal, or other damages. The author takes full responsibility for the contents of this book. Amsterdam Academy Press is not responsible for the content (including images), nor owns this content. For any questions about the content, please reach out to the author directly. This is a new edition of a book originally published in paperback by United P.C., London in 2020 under the title *Who's the Villain?*.

ISBN paperback 978-90-834057-6-6

Self-publishing powered by
Amsterdam Academy Press
www.amsterdamacademy.com

Acknowledgements

I would like to thank the following people for their perseverance with myself and the creation of this book:

AMSTERDAM ACADEMY PRESS
Hannah Huber – Founder of Amsterdam Academy Press
Anna Trapmore – Editor and Proofreader
Cigdem Guven – Cover Designer
Lisa Hall – Layout Guru

HMP PRISONS
To all the staff who helped me rehabilitate and find focus in my life. Special thanks to Ian in the music department at HMP The Mount.

THE KOESTLER AWARDS
For giving me the confidence to finish my autobiography

FINDING RHYTHMS
Robin Harris and his amazing team

Thomas Newton – for standing by me and believing in me when everyone else turned their backs.

AMY-PETER-MELISSA-KAYDEN-KAYNE
BONNIE-RAY

I took this photo while serving time at HMP The Mount in Hertfordshire, on a camera that had been smuggled into the prison. Turning my cell into a study caused a bit of a stir with the guards – and with my fellow inmates – but no matter what anyone said, I was determined to get the job done.

"Virtues should not be silently ignored, while the perpetrators of wrong actions should be threatened with disgrace before posterity."
Tacitus, 56 AD–c.120

Introduction

"Is he always this polite?"

It's the summer of '91 and I've just arrived at the Jericho Tavern to catch Macca – the manager of this Oxford music venue – mid-argument with one of the barmaids.

There I am, one of most important cassette tapes of the twentieth century quite literally in the palm of my hand, but I barely get acknowledged as I offer it to him.

"Give it to *her*," he says with a snarl as he storms off.

The drummer from The Blue Fields later told me Macca was putting it about that he was the one who discovered Radiohead – that he gave them the break they so desperately needed. Whatever. He almost got the band's three-track demo bounced off the back of his head that day.

It's a good job I kept my cool.

You've heard of Radiohead, of course. You've heard of Thom Yorke. If you're a fan, you probably know all about the band's meteoric rise to fame after being discovered at The Jericho Tavern in Oxford. You may know all of this, yet you will have no idea who I am.

Radiohead did not just fall from the sky – there is a beginning to this story and our beginning is not at The Jericho Tavern. Sure, The Tavern is where they got picked up – and I take full credit for that. Have I ever been given any credit? Well, you're reading this and you already have the answer.

Some say that everyone has a skeleton in their closet. I am most definitely Radiohead's.

Thom and the band had no choice but to leave me behind and do their very best to forget about me. I can't really blame them for that. I was on the cusp of something great and I blew it.

I couldn't control myself. I started taking drugs – lots of drugs. I let the Es, speed and coke consume me and I made some stupid choices. Deeper and deeper I spiralled, and with that came the thieving and cheating. The drug dealing started slowly at first, then with the money and the drugs came the wild parties.

Thom wrote *Just*, off the album *The Bends*, about someone close to him who was hell-bent on self-destruction. I am that someone. Radiohead's 1996 interview with Matt Pinfield (on MTV's *120 Minutes*) sheds more light on the situation, but I believe that was the first and last time Thom ever made reference to myself in an interview. In song though? Well, that's another story.

The Jericho Tavern, on Walton Street in Oxford – a great music venue 'On a Friday'. The band changed their name to Radiohead not long after their legendary gig here in 1991.

Radiohead. A great name for a band, don't you think? And Thom. Not your classic, everyday spelling, 'Tom' – it had to be 'Thom'.

That 'h' makes all the difference. The manipulation of a single word or letter can change so much in a statement, a story, a song.

Let's see. 'Get on one, kidda' – a simple saying back in the 1990s, when the rave scene hit Middle England. The youth of Oxford joined the madness, as did I.

The phrase was used by many of my fellow partygoers. It refers to taking ecstasy, 'Get on one' meaning an E, and 'kidda', a slang word for a mate, a friend. I printed it on the back of my hoodie. I thought it looked cool (well, it was the 90s).

"What does 'kidda' mean?" Thom asked me one evening.

"It means mate, friend," I replied.

GET ON ONE, KIDDA..... **KID A**

And there you have it – the title of Radiohead's fourth album.

"So, what?" I can imagine you asking yourselves. "Thom has used something you said, big deal."

I challenged the administrators at the fansite www.greenplastic.com over the same comment and, after further discussing my involvement with Radiohead, I was blocked from their forum. The reason given? "Blocked because we can't handle the truth". I love the fact that they gave a reason for blocking me, but mostly, I admire their honesty.

Thom's talent for manipulating words is what started me writing this autobiography.

One day, in the summer of '91, Thom returned from Oxford City Centre to the pub and restaurant where I worked in Buckland Village. He seemed concerned at, what he thought, was the waste of young lives.

He had been at uni for a couple of years so he hadn't been aware that a lot of the Oxford youth had made the decision to drop out and live the life of a nomad. They were labelled 'travellers' but not in the same sense as gypsies. These kids were having a good time – free and away from the stresses of normal life – living in old, converted buses and travelling the country, going from party to party.

Thom told me he was surprised by how many "dropouts", as he called them, he had seen in Oxford's centre, sitting around in Magdalene Square, drinking and getting stoned.

He brought out his old red leather-bound journal, the type you could imagine Lawrence of Arabia having with him. He had written a collection of lyrics about these young kids in Magdalene Square. At the time, they had no real structure – just a jumble of scribbled words – but this later became the basis for the track *Let Down* off the album *OK Computer*.

I was also a prolific poet back then, writing short stories, songs and lyrics. Thom and I were inseparable at this time in our lives, swapping stories and sharing inspirations, so I gave him a collection of notebooks and folders to look at, filled with what I considered to be my 'Works of Art'. When he left that afternoon, he took the notebooks with him.

Apart from Radiohead's first album, *Pablo Honey*, I have again and again found my work on almost every one of their albums. No matter how Thom manipulates a word or two, it's still my work.

Now before you go off on some rant about who the hell do I think I am for writing this and how desperate and mean I must be, please bear in mind that such tracks as *High and Dry*, *Where I End and You Begin*, *Myxomatosis* and many more, were not originally written by Thom.

To give you a sense of what I'm saying, here are a few tracks from three of Radiohead's albums, all of which contain lyrics or poetry that I wrote. You will also see the slight manipulation of words that I have mentioned earlier. Remember, this is still the introduction and I can assure you that this really is just the tip of the iceberg. When I am released from prison, I will focus my attention on the rest of Radiohead's albums. Who knows what I will find.

Where I End and You Begin, off the album *Hail to the Thief*, released June 2003, was originally entitled *Where They End and We Begin*. I wrote this poem back in the summer of 1991. It was my way of explaining how the DNA in our bodies is essentially the same DNA left behind after the demise of the dinosaurs, hence *Where They End and We Begin*.

In the song *Street Spirit (Fade Out)*, from the album *The Bends*, the lyrics "*Fade out, fade out again*" were not intended to be lyrics at all. Thom had read them as such, when in actual fact they were nothing more than a reminder to myself. I had written a series of poetic stanzas about my hometown of Skelmersdale in Lancashire. At the end of each stanza, the last word was to be repeated until it faded out into the distance, just like a record would do. First stanza complete, and I wrote "fade out" in the margins. Second stanza complete, and I wrote "fade out again", and so on.

Subterranean Homesick Alien, off the album *OK Computer*, came about after an encounter I had late one night on Buckland Road in Oxfordshire. I'll tell you more about this later. I told Thom all about it at the time. Should I choose my next word carefully? I think not – PLAGIARISED.

Dismiss me as a crank or a crackpot, I've put up with that for years, so it doesn't bother me anymore. I am not afraid of Radiohead or their lawyers.

I bet you Radiohead purists hate my fuckin guts already. That may be the case, but please keep in mind that this is my life, and I can tell my story, my way. Thom will no doubt have his own version of events. You will not get to hear Thom's side of this story because he cannot argue with the truth. If his lawyers have anything to say about it, I welcome their challenge. But nothing will be said; this is a can of worms that they will not want to lift the lid off. There will be no statements released, no legal challenge – zip, zero. I think that they would call that behaviour dignified silence; where I come from, we call it cowardice.

During 1994 to 1995, I was convinced that the police were watching me. Through my own investigation and research, I am one hundred per cent convinced that Thom hired a private detective to track me down, take pictures of me and then trick his way into my apartment under the guise of a Victim Support Worker. Again, I'll explain more later but my point is: I am sure that if I spied on someone, then sneaked my way into their house, I would be labelled a stalker and dealt with by the authorities. Paying someone to do your dirty work for you is no different, other than the fact that you haven't got the balls to do it yourself.

In September 2013, I sent a short letter to Thom's father, letting him know that I was writing this memoir and asking him to inform his son of my whereabouts so his lawyers, if they so wished, could contact me to discuss this matter. Thom then took the letter to his lawyers, Statham Gill Davies. They did their very best to shut me up with the help of the Public Protection Department at HMP Swaleside, where I was serving a ten-year sentence for importing drugs into the United Kingdom.

Statham Gill Davies (SGD) not only failed to silence me, I believe that they have failed Thom and the band. I am a convicted drug trafficker with a lot to say. Why on earth would anyone want to be associated with this, socially or artistically?

Several times I had tried to communicate with SGD. They issued me with a No Contact request, in respect of Mr Thom Yorke, like I was some sort of crackpot superfan who was nothing more than a perpetual nuisance. Considering that I had made no attempt to contact Thom or the band (not ever) since we went our separate ways back in late 1991, I found their behaviour not only bizarre, it was yet another kick in the balls. The saying 'red rag to a bull' comes to mind.

I became even more determined to publish this story. I sent a seventy-page synopsis to SGD in December 2013, entitled *Memoir of a Rock 'n' Roll Criminal*, the prelude to this autobiography. Well, they went ape shit. They threatened the Public Protection Team at HMP Swaleside with all kinds of legal action if I contacted them again, ordering me to communicate with them only through a legal representative.

The Public Protection Team didn't have a clue what to do with me. They first blocked all my mail in and out of the prison. I had to get my solicitor to write to them, complaining about the action that they had taken.

A couple of days later and I was frogmarched down to the Custodial Manager's office on E-wing. I was faced with the Head of Security, Seconded Probation and the Public Protection Team. At first they tried to play hardball to scare me into silence.

Yer, mate, that worked.

I didn't crumble despite their overwhelming presence. I remained calm and composed which threw them a little. They were no doubt expecting me to fly off the handle. Seconded Probation finally conceded that, as this was an historic matter, they, the Ministry of Justice, could not be party to any grievance that I had with Radiohead or their lawyers. They then politely asked me not to contact Statham Gill Davies again until I left HMP Swaleside. To this, I agreed.

The next afternoon when I came back from my work placement at DHL, ten weeks' worth of mail – incoming and outgoing – had been thrown across my bed. All of it had been opened and no doubt copied and read.

I can fully understand Statham Gill Davies not wanting to talk to me. Fighting a lengthy legal battle on behalf of Radiohead would see them reap vast rewards, win or lose, protecting their client. But all that they had to do was talk to me, and this memoir could have remained in the closet where they no doubt believe it belongs.

HMP Swaleside, one of Britain's toughest jails. It has a real bad reputation throughout the prison system but I excelled here, making friends quickly and pushing myself every day to re-educate. All the staff gave me one hundred percent – and they encouraged me to continue with my education at my next prison, HMP The Mount in Hertfordshire.

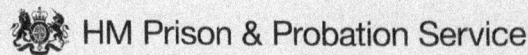 HM Prison & Probation Service

OFFICIAL

Notice to Prisoner– Restriction of Communications

Prisoner Details					
Forename	Surname	Date of Birth (DD/MM/YYYY)	Prison Number	Establishment	Cell Location
PAUL	MCCARTHY	20/11/1967	AG20346	HMP SWALESIDE	E34

Restricted Person Details	
Forename	Surname
THOM	YORKE

Dear Paul McCarthy..

You have been restricted from contacting the above-mentioned person on the following ground(s):

Restriction Details		
Time period	Form of Contact	Grounds for Restriction (Prison Rule 34)
26/01/2013	NONE	34.-(1) the secretary of state may, with a view to securing discipline and good order or the prevention of crime or in the interests of any persons, impose restrictions, either generally or in a case, upon the letters or other communications to be permitted between a prisoner and other persons.

The decision to restrict you from contacting this individual has not been taken lightly as our establishment is committed to maintaining ties with family and friends.

Restriction of communications is not part of any form of punishment, but we are committed to make our establishment a safe and secure environment for prisoners, visitors, and staff and to safeguard the public where necessary. The restriction will be reviewed on (insert date).

You may appeal against this decision by using: (delete as applicable)

- The Formal Complaints procedure available on your residential unit for the attention of the Head of Security and Operations.

Notification of Restriction Version 2.1 – Issued January 2024

Now, if you are a Radiohead purist, you are going to hate what I am about to say: I am Radiohead's first true fan. No one can ever take that away from me, not anyone. From the moment that I first listened to Thom's three-track demo back in 1990, I was hooked. I really admire him for all his achievements – and I think that the band are as good today as they have always been – but the contents of this memoir has messed with my head for years.

Since 1995, I have had to suffer in silence as my poetry was spewed back at me in many different ways. No matter where I was, when I heard a track by Radiohead that contained my work, no matter how small a part may have been used, it fuckin tore a hole inside me that would lead to absolute self-loathing. With this came the self-medication.

No one believed a word that I said – and how on earth could I challenge Thom about any of this? The best thing for me to do was to remain drugged out of my head.

On most nights after seeing or hearing my work I would drink, smoke pot and do crack cocaine. I would take Valium or diazepam until I passed out. For years I was a mess, mentally and physically.

Thanks to Her Majesty's Prison Service, I am now as clean as a whistle and, without doubt, focused. I came into prison having never completed a single exam. Being dyslexic and leaving school at fourteen, I had no qualifications at all. Since being in prison, I have achieved: Level 3 English, Level

3 Maths, ICT Level 4, a B-Tech in Sound Engineering, a City and Guilds in Music Technology, also several Gateway courses – but my favourite achievement was winning Gold at the Koestler Arts Annual Awards.

Memoir of a Rock 'n' Roll Criminal – a synopsis of this book – was voted Best In Category for Nonfiction and True Life – and having Grayson Perry on the panel of judges making a decision over my work really did give me the confidence to believe in myself and to continue along this path, no matter how painful or uncomfortable it may become.

Thom and the band will never give me the credit that I deserve, so I will just have to take it. I have no fear of Statham Gill Davies. Let's see them silence me when this book is all over the internet. I will sit in court, any court – and with Thom in the dock.

Don't make me laugh.

What I will do is tell this story as truthfully as possible. At times I will take into consideration people's positions and/or their feelings. I will change some names and places to protect both the innocent and the guilty. If you are not mentioned in this memoir, don't think that you're not important to me. I may have left you out because you have moved on and may not want to be connected to me in any way – or perhaps I have left you out because you're a scumbag. Make up your own mind on that one.

I would like to point out that it's not my intention to

discredit anyone, but it's going to be hard not to, as much of what I write will at times make Thom and Edward look like the baddies. That's because their behaviour has been rather unsporting. They have brought this on themselves.

I have suffered for my crimes. I have done many things wrong and I've paid the price. Just because Radiohead are Radiohead and they have a fantastic legal team, it does not mean that they are above the law. That's my point entirely: no one is above the law.

So, to conclude this introduction: proof. What proof do I have to substantiate this story? Well, that remains to be seen, but I will tell you this: Thom and his lawyers will not at any time challenge this autobiography. If you – yes you – wrote this story, the shit would most definitely hit the fan because you were not there. I was, and this story is about me and the nonsense I have had to put up with for years. So, Radiohead, come and have a go if you think you're "honest" enough. It's time I brushed myself off, unlock this prison cell one last time and finally face the music.

JUST - Track 7 - The Bends
One day I'll get to you
And teach you how to get
To purist hell
You did it to yourself, you did
And that's what really hurts
You did it to yourself
(Sorry, slight manipulation)

Thom and the band could not have been further from my mind. Here I am, May 2003, things were going great as far as I was concerned. I was back in Skelmersdale after yet another trip to Spain. I was involved in trafficking all kinds throughout Europe: cigarettes, hash, money, cocaine, heroin – it didn't matter to me. At this point in my life, I was only interested in making money and how I got it was my own business. If someone got hurt, so what? If I went to prison, big deal.

Twelve years of drugs and parties and I thought that I was something special. Overweight, greasy skin and, from time to time, I would suffer the most hideous blood-filled cysts popping through my scalp. They would appear under the skin and slowly grow into small balloons. The hair would then fall out, the cyst huge and disgusting for the world to see. I bought a scalpel and performed my own surgery, only when I was out of my nut after a crack binge.

The things that you do to yourself when you're a junkie are mind-blowing. The fear of everything becomes so blurred. You forget to be scared and just get on with slicing open your scalp and forcing out the filth. The relief that I felt afterwards was amazing. Satisfied that I had completed the task, I would again begin to smoke crack. No doubt, weeks later, I would have another blood-filled cyst to deal with.

Oh, I was definitely something special.

To be honest, I hated myself; I hated what I had become. The missed opportunities – along with the fact that I had let so many good people slip through my fingers due to nothing more than my own selfishness. Blah, blah, blah. We will get back to self-pity a little later.

I was earning good money, so I could afford to pay a cleaner to come around and sort my house out for when I returned.

This particular night would change my attitude to Thom and the band in a way that I never thought possible. Janine, my cleaner, was still finishing off the house when I got home earlier that evening. Before I got back, I first called in to my mate's house in Liverpool and I collected a couple of grams of cocaine. He warned me that it was strong stuff and that I should go easy with it. He knew that I was trying my best to get my head together. The trips to Europe were helping me to stay clean, as I had no choice out there but to stay straight.

I asked Janine if she wanted to spend the night with me. She didn't say no, and I knew where the bag of coke would lead us. Why not? We were both single. I asked her if she would go to the shops and buy a couple of bottles of wine. As she was leaving, I noticed Jonathan Ross on the TV doing his usual 'take the piss out of the Green Room' routine. He then mentioned that Radiohead would be playing tracks from their forthcoming album, *Hail to the Thief*. Nice one, I thought, *I'll watch that*.

Janine left for the shops and I went upstairs to take a shower. When I came back down, she was sitting on the couch, two bottles of wine in front of her on the table. I took out the bag of coke and cut a few lines on a CD sleeve. I then took the wine to the kitchen and put it into the fridge. I could hear Janine snorting like a pig. When I walked back into the living room, she was giving herself that famous cocaine users' two-fingered clean-up. That's where you pinch both your nostrils with your thumb and forefinger while sniffing up rapidly – firstly so that you don't have any evidence on your face but, more importantly, so that you don't waste any.

"Janine," I said. "That's really strong stuff, it's not the same shite you buy round here."

"Oh, behave yourself, Paul. I've had it loads of times."

Well it wasn't long before she had a face like a smacked arse.

"Janine, Radiohead's coming on. I don't want you pulling faces all the way through it. Go upstairs and splash some cold water on your face."

As she huffed and puffed her way up the stairs, I snorted a little line. My drug problem was almost over, now I was only using on the odd weekend. It was a far cry from the nights spent smoking crack and taking Valium.

Following through on my earlier offer, I had no choice but to go upstairs and rescue Janine. As we made our way back down the stairs, I could see the TV from across the living room, and there it was, like a good kick in the nuts. The title of Radiohead's first song flashed up on the screen: *Where I End and You Begin*. I froze, my eyes glued to the TV. I recognised the title immediately.

Janine, on seeing me dumfounded asked, "What's wrong, Paul?"

I then heard the word 'dinosaur'.

"You little prick," I said out loud.

Janine again asked, "Paul, what's wrong?"

"Never mind Janine, just put something else on."

"But Paul, I thought that you liked them?"

I tried to settle in for the night, but it was no use. Yet again, after all these years, Thom still had the ability to fuck with my head. After a couple of lines, I was in the kitchen with a spoon and a packet of bicarbonate of soda.

Janine stood behind me and said, "Paul, if you do that, I am going home."

Thank fuck she was there because I would have gone on a binge and a half. I couldn't stop thinking about Thom. *Where I End and You Begin*… all the old feelings came flooding back: rejection, betrayal, all washed down with a good measure of self-pity.

I had stopped talking about the band years before. People would look right through me at the very mention of Radiohead – or I would suffer a barrage of verbal abuse from the local wannabe gangsters who I was knocking about with.

Back in 2000, I was working with a lad from Liverpool. We were sitting in the Fiveways pub at the end of Queens Drive in Liverpool with about a dozen up-and-coming local gangsters in our company. The lad who I worked with had known me for some time. He knew all about my involvement with Radiohead.

One of the other lads said out loud, "I've just read a sound book about Radiohead."

Little did I know that my so-called mate had put him up to it.

I looked at the lad and said, "I used to be friends with Thom Yorke. I promoted the band back in the 90s."

Everyone went quiet and the lad I was with says, "See what I have to fuckin put up with."

No one laughed or said a word. A couple of them just looked at me like I was a fuckin dickhead. That was it, right there. That's when I made the conscious decision never to mention that fuckin band in public again. From that moment, I kept all my thoughts and my agonies to myself. I put the past behind me, and I moved on.

Well, at least that's what I thought.

After the Jonathan Ross incident, I went out and bought two of Radiohead's albums: *OK Computer*, and the one that had just recently sent my head back a few years, *Hail to the Thief*. I still checked the credits to see if I had a mention. Stupid, I know.

I knew that I would soon be leaving the United Kingdom to continue my illegal activities abroad. I decided that it was about time that I started paying attention. I found myself obsessing, playing every song, over and over again, so that I could listen to every word that Thom said. With every new revelation I became more and more determined to write this story. This is my third attempt (the last two manuscripts I burnt because I was afraid that the authorities would find them and use them against me if I was caught doing what I was doing).

The lyrics and the artwork on *OK Computer* really messed my head up – just like *The Bends* had before it. ARTWORK! Yes, the artwork, the inlay to the album. On *OK Computer* there is a cut-out of an underground/overground railway station showing three characters – two to the right and one to the left. I'm convinced that this is a depiction of my so-called accidental meeting with Edward O'Brien and producer David Smith in the underpass of Didcot train station.

Similarly, the sketch 'I AM CANARY WHARF' – on the inlay for *The Bends* – came about after a 'chance' meeting with Thom, on Abingdon Road in Oxford. As I'll explain later, that meeting would also go on to inspire the creation of the track *The Tourist*, off the album *OK Computer*.

The Bends also features a photo of someone standing in front of a double window. The picture's blurred but I'm 100 per cent sure that this is the photo taken of me by the 'Victim Support' worker who came to my apartment in 1994. To be continued.

I had to try and forget what went on between us. It was not doing my mental health any good. For years, so much of my poetry and my lyrics had been used by the band and not a soul on earth believed a word I said. Seeing my poem *Where They End and We Begin* transformed into one of Radiohead's so-called creations – and, once again, not a mention of me in any of the credits – set me right back.

Before, when people would look right through me at the very mention of Thom or the band, I would curl up inside, unable to truly convey the truth. That's because I was weak – not physically, but mentally. I was taking a shitload of drugs to mask the putrid feelings that I had inside. Don't think for one minute that I am blaming Thom for my drug use – that was my choice – but I tell you this: the choices he made with regards to my work – and his failure to credit me or to thank me in any way – left me disappointed, bewildered and, most of all, confused. Confused because I didn't know how to deal with the feelings that I was having, and I knew in my heart that I had never done anything to hurt him.

When I listened to the song *Sulk* I couldn't believe that he would take our most intimate conversations and use them in a song. I told Thom about my childhood. How it was difficult with my dad in prison. During this time a few things happened that changed me forever.

Nye Bevan Swimming Pool opened while my dad was inside. My mum was out of her nut on the couch after being prescribed Valium by the doctor. I convinced her to give me 50p so that I could go to the pool with all the other kids. She handed me the money and I grabbed a towel and ran up the path for about a mile, trying to catch up with Callum and his big sister, but they had gone in ahead of me. I then convinced the girl at the kiosk to let me in. I went into the changing rooms alone and, being a little scared, I didn't take my Y-fronts off. I changed into my swimming trunks, put my clothes inside the locker and made my way to the poolside.

At the deep end the kids were running and jumping in. Never in my life had I been in a swimming pool. I walked to the edge and I could see the bottom. It didn't look deep at all. I stepped back against the wall, pushed myself off and just like the other kids, I ran and jumped in the deep end. I only remember floating around in a green cloud. I don't recall any sound at all, just my whole body as if running inside this green cloud.

The next thing that I remember is being resuscitated and coming round inside the first aid room. For years, two things have puzzled me about this. Firstly, I was never taken to hospital – and why on earth did the girl at the kiosk let a five-year-old kid in unaccompanied? It was the 70s, I suppose.

Thom seems to have an infatuation with drowning, as seen in the video for *No Surprises* – track 10 off the album *OK Computer*. To me, this felt directly related to my drowning. When I first saw the video for *No Surprises* I shouted at the TV, "It's my life Thom, not yours!".

That day at the pool, my cousin Michael saw me being resuscitated and he called his dad to come and collect me. My skin was a sort of pale green. To this day I don't know why. I said to Uncle Morris: "Is my skin green because I was in that cloud?"

He obviously had no idea what I was going on about. He just said to me, "No lad. That's because of the lack of oxygen in your blood."

I was only a little kid, so while my dad was in prison I would sleep in my mother's bed and listen to her cry herself to sleep every night. I would climb over her and cuddle her while wiping the tears from her eyes.

Having made it to my teenage years, I went through a period of emotional meltdown.

I couldn't believe it when my mate Chris Fields died. We were not close at first – he was trying to steal my girlfriend Katrina off me – but after some time we became friends. We were at the local disco one Friday night, drinking whisky and smoking Hamlet cigars, pretending to strangers that we were from London and had just moved to Skem. Then just like that, the following Sunday, he was dead.

A few weeks later, Catherine Williams and Paula Fazakerly stopped me outside Saint Edmund's School. Catherine put her arms around me and said, "Paul, I'm going into hospital tomorrow to have an operation on my kidneys. Can I have a kiss for good luck?"

I gently pushed her away and said, "You can have as many kisses as you want when you come back," – and I meant it. Catherine was lovely.

She died a couple of days later.

Julie Masterton's death also affected me badly. The day before she went into hospital, she sat in her doorway singing *Tell Laura I Love Her*. Julie and Catherine had both died due to complications after surgery. Both suffered with kidney problems.

Fake Plastic Trees, track 4 off the album *The Bends*, contains the lyrics "He used to do surgery for girls in the 80s, but gravity always wins". And it certainly did.

But before Chris and Julie and Catherine came the death of my friend Eric Wilson. That fucked my head right up. I sat in my room for about three weeks. I was convinced that I was next, it just seemed to me that everyone around me was dying. I sank into a weird depression, writing poetry and songs – I suppose as a way of trying to deal with it all. The things that I wrote about were not normal for a kid my age.

I listened to The Doors and The Cure, over and over. I was truly lost inside myself. Just hearing my parents shout my name up the stairs was driving me crazy. I wanted to be left alone. The idea of talking to someone made me angry. I was sure that I was about to die. I sat every night in my bedroom waiting for it. In my mind I would call it on.

Then Katrina, who I had been close to since I was about six, came round to our house with her knickers in a twist because she hadn't seen me for so long. I had to put a brave face on and go and meet her that evening. We sat in the park and I repeatedly sung songs to her by The Cure. She asked me over and over what was going on. I couldn't tell her. I couldn't tell anyone. I was so emotional at this point that I could cry on the spot. I would look in the mirror and, within seconds, my face would redden and the tears of anger would begin to flow. Katrina's constant attention brought me back to reality – but something else was about to cast a cloud over my teenage years – something that would trouble me for a very long time and trigger a web of lies.

When I was 17, I found out that I was going to be a dad. Things went well with Kathy for a while but then, through my own selfishness, I left before our baby was born. I moved down South and didn't speak to her – or see our son Peter – for two years.

I began telling people I had a son, but I lied about what had happened, saying that Peter lived with his grandma because his mum had haemorrhaged and died soon after giving birth. Well, I used this lie many times – I even used my grief over Eric's death to give my story a bit of credibility (I know, shameful, isn't it?).

I'm happy to say that Kathy and I eventually worked things out, and that we kept in touch for our son's sake – but back then I wasn't ready to share this story, not even with my closest friends.

I told Thom my odd, made-up version of events one night when we were smoking pot and drinking at The Lamb Inn bar. I wanted to say what had really happened with Peter – to explain how devastated I was about it all – but it took me a long time to face the truth and get myself properly together.

All the other stuff came out though, over several nights at the bar: my friends' deaths, my dad going to prison, the day I nearly died at the pool. I told him how it all weighed heavy on my mind. Being a little drunk and stoned, we both got a bit emotional throughout these evenings and opened our hearts to one another. As I was the one who was building the spliffs all the time, I occasionally paused to burn the hash for the next spliff and I remember telling him how much it still hurt me, having to see my mum cry herself to sleep every night, how it really affected me and how I found it hard to trust people because they always betray you or leave you behind.

Thom, seeing that I was upset, said to me: "Paul, you're the only real friend that I have. You're the only person I know who doesn't want anything from me. I promise you that I won't forget you."

Now, here in the song *Sulk*, track 11 off *The Bends*, are my innermost emotions spewed back at me:

Sometimes you sulk
Sometimes you burn
God rest your soul
When the loving comes
And we're already gone
Just like your dad
You'll never change

By the time this song appeared on the album, I had been in the Oxford Mail Newspaper for the burglary of a computer factory and I had spent three weeks in Brixton prison. So yes, just like my dad, I had resorted to crime. The only difference was that he stole to put food on the table; I stole because I was a dumb-arse lazy fuck who couldn't be bothered sorting his head out and getting a job. I was just like one of the travellers that Thom was on about in his song *Let Down* – I dropped out. *Just like your dad you'll never change.* Oh, fuck me. I was so angry when I heard that song. And don't get me started on how I felt about the cover for *The Bends*.

The creation of this album cover is, for me, one of the most disturbing things Thom put together. Given my near-death experience at Nye Bevan swimming pool, you can see why I was haunted by this image – a green-tinged CPR mannequin that Thom and his artist friend found and filmed in a hospital resuscitation room. Back when the album was released, I was fully involved with drugs and using daily. I found it difficult and upsetting to deal with whatever Radiohead seemed to be throwing at me. It felt like a personal attack – like having my life played out without being involved or having any say-so. I carried this image around in my head for years.

Thankfully, I am not on drugs anymore and I am sure that there's a lot of you out there who still want to dismiss me as a liar. If that's the case, feel free to put this book aside. If my accusations make you angry, please don't be. I am not angry anymore. Thom using my life and the events that shaped me comes as no surprise. He didn't have much of a life, sheltered in that little village. He was petrified of his father and of his own appearance, the operations that he had on his eye.

All of this held him back – not academically, but socially. He really did feel like an outcast when we met. I don't care what anyone says about me for writing any of this. I brought out the best in Thom and I gave him the confidence to face many of his demons. I was brash and cocky to the point of being a little too forward, but I always remained kind and curious. This got me ahead as a young man. Obviously, because there I was at twenty-four running a two-million-pound bar and restaurant.

The Lamb Inn at Buckland Village in Oxfordshire is where our story takes off and, for me, with all the ecstasy and the speed that I was taking, well, I took off like a rocket.

In the early 90s I was the manager at the Oxfordshire pub, and this is where I first got to know Edward. He soon sent Thom my way. From the moment Thom and I first met we were inseparable. I gave him friendship, kindness and support, the like he had never known.

Back then the band was called 'On a Friday'. Thom told me they had chosen that name because it was the only time that they seemed to get together. The band had only done one gig (at the Rock Garden in London's Covent Garden) before we met. Now Thom, trusting me the way that he did, handed me the band's three-track demo and, soon after, I was pounding the streets of Oxford and London booking gigs and creating a buzz with the record companies.

Thom told me, "We're all over the place at the moment, no one's got any real direction."

"So, what you're saying is, you all need a good kick up the arse?"

"Yes Paul, that's exactly what we need."

I was only too happy to oblige and yet the more I carried out Thom's wishes, the more Edward grew to hate me.

What I did, I did for Thom. I didn't care too much for the others. How could I? I didn't really know them. As for Edward, well, he ran hot and cold, so getting along with him always seemed a challenge. After a while, I just thought that he was a bit of a prick. You will find out a little later why the problems started with me and Edward. It wasn't just because Thom and I were friends.

With my help, the band rose quickly into the world of music. I, on the other hand, rose quickly into a world of drugs and drug dealing. Eventually I was trafficking millions of pounds' worth of illegal items all over Europe. I am now writing this in a Dutch jail, coming to the end of my twelve-year prison sentence: ten years in the United Kingdom for importing heroin, and two years in Holland for money laundering.

Someone asked me, when I was back in HMP Lancaster Farms in the UK, "You are going straight when you get out, Scouse?" To which I replied, "Yer, straight round to my mates, to get another ten kilos."

I was only joking of course.

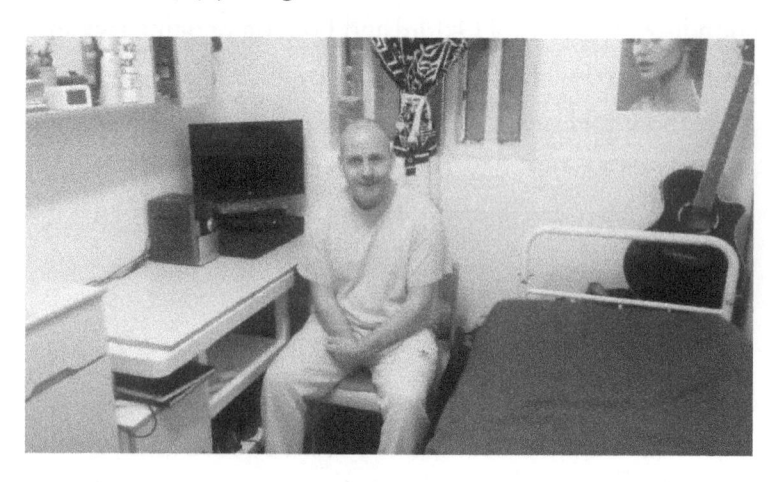

Yours truly serving time. I worked out that within five years, I was moved to sixteen different prisons.

First, I would like to take you back a little, to help you understand Thom's motive for writing some of his songs. I won't bore you to death with too much information. I will keep this section as brief as possible. It is vital that you get to grips with the kind of person I was when Thom and I became friends.

I haven't always been a criminal. Before I met Thom, I was already carrying a certain amount of emotional baggage. He has used many parts of my life and he has focused on some of our most intimate conversations.

To help you understand his music and his words, I think it's best that you understand where I came from, and how I ended up fortunate enough to be a part of Thom's life. If you are a Radiohead fan, then you may see a lot of comparisons to myself throughout his songs and videos. I am not going to point out everything that I've come across over the years, but when you understand my relationship with him, you'll be in a better position to draw your own conclusions.

Thanks Paul, how difficult is that? *Thanks Paul* – the only two words that I've ever wanted to see in print or maybe hear during an interview. So many times over the years I have asked myself why. What I did, I did to myself, I have never blamed anyone for the choices that I made. Hurt myself? Yes, I did, many times over. Did I ever hurt Thom or the band? No, not ever.

My time with them ended in late 1991, after their first gig at the Old Fire Station in Oxford City Centre. I only ever called Thom's parents' house once after that, a couple of weeks later. I hadn't seen Thom for a while, his mother told me that he was out of the country. I remember thinking then that I wouldn't be seeing him again. I made no attempt to contact any of them, not ever. I was in the wrong, I knew that, and I stayed well away.

In February 1993, when *Pablo Honey* was due to be released, I couldn't wait to get my hands on a copy – even though I had resigned myself to the fact that I would not be seeing Thom again, I still felt connected to him. Oxford was abuzz with talk of this great new band. Just before the album's release, Thom's father came into the bar with his younger son Andy, gloating about how well Thom and the band were doing. This really pissed me off because, just a few months before, he was giving me a bit of a talking to, saying that I should stop filling Thom's head with this music nonsense.

Anyway, the release date was upon us. I was certain that I would finally see my name on a record. I was so sure of myself – a thank-you at least. I rushed into Oxford and made my way to the HMV Music Store on the high street. I bought the CD and I stood outside, scrambling to tear off the plastic wrapper. I couldn't contain myself. I pulled out the inlay, surely my name would be in the credits? Again and again I flicked through the pages. I must have missed something. I went back to the front page of the inlay and slowly, page by page, I looked for the smallest of writing in a hope I would find some reference to myself. Did I miss something? Maybe I did!

Since I was eleven years old, I was hell-bent on being a poet, a rock star or even an actor. My three older brothers and I were all born in the 1960s. They filled the house with music: Ian Dury and the Blockheads, David Bowie, The Eagles, Janis Joplin, Jimi Hendrix, Joy Division, Echo and the Bunnymen. With four boys in the house, there had to be a record or two by the Sex Pistols. I can even remember a record by R. Dean Taylor, although I think that one may have belonged to our mother.

Music to me was electrifying; where did all these people come from? Artists back then seemed full of mystery and excitement. People talked about Jim Morrison, Hendrix and Joplin with real love and compassion. At such a young age, I was aware that these artists were dead – but the way that my brothers and their friends spoke about these people somehow made me feel as if they knew them.

My brother Andy and his mate Les Martin smoked some pot one night and they went on and on about Ian Curtis from the band Joy Division. These artists had been dead for a good few years, and yet here they were being spoken about in such high regard. To me, it was as if they had a God-like status.

Morrison Hotel by The Doors took pride of place in my eldest brother John's record collection. I remember returning home from school one afternoon, I could hear the music coming from the back kitchen. When I opened the dining-room door, I could see a stack of LPs leaning on the leg of the open-top record player, and at the front of them all was the cover of this album. I took a few steps towards it, focusing on Jim Morrison looking back at me.

"Don't touch that!"

John's voice scared the shit out of me. He was standing right behind me.

That's the first time I ever saw a Doors record. Like so many other kids before and since, I was hooked. I would copy every word that Jim said, taking the needle back and forth so that I could learn every song, line by line. This wasn't only confined to The Doors. I did this with every record that I could find. The whole 60s/ early-70s vibe was well and truly embedded in my psyche.

At the age of five, I was performing *Long Haired Lover from Liverpool* by Jimmy Osmond for my nan and Aunt Rose, wearing my flared jeans and leather-pleated platform shoes. I would sing and dance for anyone, believing that I would one day be a star. I went through every trend as a teenager. One of my greatest inspirations back in the 80s was my old mate Eric Parker. He was the last Teddy Boy on Earth, mad for rock 'n' roll music. He also loved UB40. I would babysit his four boys and when he and his wife Teresa came home, I would either be playing one of his many albums or I would be twanging away on my guitar. I would write songs with about six verses and two or three choruses.

Eric stopped me one night and said, "Listen lad, don't suffocate the song with a million words. Keep it simple for the kids to learn."

With poetic advice like that, I was sure that I was going to be famous.

As a teenager, movies like *Quadrophenia* and *Stardust*, starring David Essex and Adam Faith, had a massive influence on me. Kids could not help but be inspired. I was a Mod, I was also a skinhead and a punk. Through every phase I dressed accordingly. Me and my mate Callum got our mothers to sew tartan strips onto our jeans back in the 70s. Bay City Rollers, great stuff.

My brothers Michael and Andrew are twins. Growing up they always protected me. Not many of the kids on the council estate where we lived had the balls to do anything to me, and if the twins ever got into any trouble, they could always rely on our eldest brother John. With three older brothers, if I had any trouble, it would be dealt with pretty sharpish. Michael can be a vicious bastard at times. Throughout my life he has helped me the most – though I'm sure that there were plenty of times he wanted to strangle the life out of me. Really though, they all looked out for me.

When I was a kid our house was full. Kids from all over Skelmersdale would turn up on motorbikes, in cars, on pushbikes. They all knew that if you needed a part for anything, one of my brothers would have it. The house was like a playground and I did my best to torment the life out of everyone who knocked on the front door. To me it was a great place to grow up.

Mum and Dad let us off the reins at a young age, but they kept us in check with the fear of a good hiding. My dad didn't fuck about with anyone. If you upset him you would get a crack. I can still hear him roaring from the living room at one of my brothers for revving the arse out of an old Lambretta or Vespa Scooter.

He treated everyone the same, even in the pub. He often fought with the other fellas in the town. The local coppers had a few black eyes from him as well. They did kick the shit out of him a few times.

John would take us all fishing, or we would hang out in the woods playing cricket and football, all the things that kids would do. Making weapons out of bamboo, darts and fishing wire was part of the fun. Michael got some fishing line with a 200lb breaking strain off another kid, and he decided to put it on his bow and arrow. Seriously, when he had finished putting it together, it was deadly. He made a flight for the arrow out of playing cards. As he was putting this together in the back square, a place behind our houses where we used to play, Ian Hamlet, who lived across from us, was sitting on his garden shed, shouting to Mick.

"That's crap that! You'll never hit anything with it."

Michael was becoming angrier by the second. He finally fitted the dart to the end of the arrow. Ian is still gobbing off at him. Mick walks into the square, points the arrow at Ian and pulls back on the bow, Ian still defiant.

"You can't hit shit with that."

Mick points it at him and lets rip. Ian has no time to react – the arrow shoots past his left ear. The flight made out of playing cards connects with his ear. The scream is horrendous. The playing cards get ripped off the arrow and they flutter to the ground. Ian, now in shock, puts his hand on his ear and screams for his mother. Michael absolutely not giving a shit, goes over to their garden gate, shouting to Ian, "Give me me fuckin arrow back," in his cheeky Scouse accent. Luckily the arrow only grazed the side of Ian's head.

It wasn't all fun and games. One of our friends Eric Wilson, who I mentioned earlier, was killed by a lad I had introduced him to just days before. I have never forgiven myself for this.

They had met up in the local pub, the Busy Bee. A group of them got into this lad's car and took off to Rainford Village. The car crashed and Eric never came home. It was a few days before his sixteenth birthday.

Mum came into my bedroom and woke me up to tell me about Eric. I didn't – or I couldn't – believe it. I ran out of the house, jumped onto my bike and went round to Michael Hilton's house. Michael stuck his head out of the top window. It was obvious that he had been crying. I asked him if it was true. I could see his lips trembling as he tried to get his words out.

"Yes, it is Paul. He's dead."

Michael shut the window and I sat outside his house. I couldn't move. I was totally confused.

From the darkened side of the roadside,
Came the shimmering lights of pain,
I long to see your smile,
But I'll never see your face again.

I was just a kid when I wrote that.

What happened with Eric kept running through my mind. There I was, sat outside his house; our other mate Harry was doing wheelies up and down the road on my bike. Eric's mum had just told us off for lifting one of the large stones off the top of the garden wall. Then the lad came walking past us, I had known him for some time. I said hello, then I introduced him to Eric while Harry was screaming his head off, doing fourteen miles per hour on my bike. The lad reached over and shook Eric's hand. As he walked off, Eric asked me.

"Who's that?"

I said, "His name's Moe Savage. He lives by my nan's."

"Ha, ha, is he a savage then?" Eric replied.

If I had not stopped to let them play on my bike that day, Moe would never have said hello and maybe Eric would still be here. I still find it hard to deal with.

I didn't see Harry again until Liverpool Football Club did the treble back in '84. I met him at Eric's graveside – we both turned up to tell him the football result. I have remained friends with Harry, but I have never told him about the introduction that I made.

Eric's grave at Saint Paul's in Skelmersdale.

Me, aged 14. This was taken at Christmas 1981, a few months before Eric died. I was not the same kid after that.

I have never been able to handle loss very well. I was five when my dad went to prison. My mum and my eldest brother told me while standing in the kitchen – I remember it as clear as day. I also knew full well where he was, despite them telling me Dad had "gone away to find work".

Mum and Dad also separated for about a year when I was eleven. I went to live with my mum on the other side of town. John, Mick and Andy stayed with my dad and the dog, Buster. I was once again gutted. From an early age, I fully understood that relationships can be, and are, painful.

John soon took off to live and work in London. Michael and Andrew both joined the British Army and went off to fight Thatcher's good fight in the Falklands. That left me in a massive house with Mum, Dad and Buster. I was bored shitless and, most of the time, it became so boring that even Buster went to live at number 147, because they had a couple of younger kids to play with. On my dad's orders, I had to go and knock on their door to get Buster to come home. If the dog felt like that, you can only imagine how I felt being alone for the first time. I hated it, the house was dreadfully quiet. This really affected me.

I quickly became a very depressed teenager. I started staying out all night with the dog. We would go to the woods and in the early hours of the night we would hang around in the pitch-black darkness by the river. We would sit for hours just listening to the sound of nature, completely un-disturbed. Then we would sneak back into the house, get some food and go back to the woods. I would make a place to sleep then, after a couple of hours, we made our way back home. Mum and Dad would ask me where I was all night. I just told them that I was at my mate's house.

This is the church doorway where I slept at night with my dog Buster. I wasn't a homeless punk, but I felt better here than I did at home. Years later I would notice a picture on the inlay of *OK Computer* showing an arched doorway with a guy facing towards it, and the caption 'SLEEP'. I don't think that this is a coincidence.

The truth was, I didn't really have any mates. I started becoming a bit of a loner. I had three girlfriends from school – Rose, Janet and Katrina – and almost every evening was spent with them. Then, when they went home I would get Buster and go back to the woods. Strange behaviour for a fourteen year old, I know. And it wasn't long before things became a lot stranger.

This is just one of the bridges that spans the River Tawd in Skelmersdale. I would spend hours with my dog Buster here in the pitch-black darkness. I returned recently at about 10pm to record a video and, I have to tell you, I was shitting myself. In my teens I didn't care at all about the dark.

It seems silly to be sentimental about a small brick wall, but this place has so many good memories for me. Day after day and night after night I would be here with Katrina, Rose, Janet and my dog Buster, smoking Regal cigarettes and drinking the occasional bottle of Cinzano Bianco.

The Twins now off being soldiers, I moved into their bedroom. Andrew had left behind two guitars. He always aspired to becoming a pop star. At one time, he had a Telecaster electric guitar, amp and microphone. I remember spying on him, through the crack in the bedroom door as he rehearsed his Ian Curtis routine.

He sold his Telecaster when he went away, but he left behind his two acoustic guitars. One of them had no D string and the other looked like it had been left out in the sun for years. Nevertheless, as I was bored out of my head, I began to teach myself how to play, obsessing over the same tune for hours on end. As I played these hypnotic, repetitive tunes, I found lyrics and poetry flowing out of me. It became easier and easier to put the lyrics to the simple, yet effective tune that I was repeating.

When Andrew came back home on leave, having heard me play what he said were "weird tunes", he started to sit and write lyrics with me. He would be writing about flowers and raindrops. I, on the other hand, would focus on car crashes and the death of rock stars. I wrote a poem about heroin when I was fourteen and how it had taken such greats as Janis Joplin, Jimi Hendrix and Elvis Presley. I know now that that's not the case but, back then, I thought all these rockers had died of a heroin overdose. I didn't even know what heroin was.

Bands started to form all around me – or that's how it seemed. Oily, a local lad and fantastic musician who was a little older than me, had a band called the B+I Ferrymen. My mate Dave Martin joined Eyes in the Sky, fronted by Peter Nelson, who I thought was the coolest guy in Skelmersdale. Peter was into bands like The Dead Kennedys, Crass, The Cramps. One day I was sitting in the park and talking to Peter and his girlfriend Vicky. She was also into punk rock and they both dressed accordingly. I told Peter that I wanted to be a punk ever since our Andy and his girlfriend took me to the Royal Court Theatre in Liverpool to watch Siouxsie and the Banshees.

Peter suggested that I should just go for it. His girlfriend also urged me to get my hair cut. She told me about a girl who had given several local punks their Mohicans.

I was convinced that night as I made my way to Linda Marr's flat in old Skelmersdale. The hair was being cut and John and Terry from the punk band Society's Problems came into the kitchen where I was having my transformation. They gave me a pair of leather ankle straps with five pyramid studs across the front, and a silver chain that fitted under the sole of your DMs.

Linda, Dead or Alive's biggest fan, and her friend Janet came in and gave me two studded arm bands and a tartan bum flap which had chains on the sides. I had already spoken to Oily about a black leather motorbike jacket that he had for sale. It cost me a fiver (five English pounds).

I made my way to Oily's house to show off my new hair style. He was so happy to see me. He called his girlfriend who brought the jacket outside. He stood me against the wall, put it on me, and called his mates out from his house. At the time they were all pot-smoking musicians. They gave me a bit of stick because the change was so dramatic – one day I looked like Nik Kershaw and now I was dressed like one of Johnny Rotten's best mates. The jacket had 200 silver studs down the left arm. The right arm was coated in red paint as if to give the impression of dripping blood. On the back was a large painted punk-rock rat, dancing to *Ooh Walla Walla* by King Kurt. 'KING KURT' was painted above the dancing rat in gold. Oily told me I looked great and that was enough for me. I couldn't wait to see Peter and Vicky.

When I did, the first thing Peter said was, "What music do you have?"

"Not much," I replied.

"Come to my mum's later," he said.

That was it. Now with a bag full of punk records, my transformation was complete.

My behaviour was becoming a bit of a concern for my parents. The dramatic change was obviously affecting people's opinions of me, and the more I was faced with confrontation, the more aggressive and disturbed I became. A group of lads from another part of town called Tanhouse chased me into Trinity School's playground and threatened to beat me up just because I was a punk. Little did they know that I had a five-inch kitchen knife inside my jacket. I pulled it out and I started screaming abuse at them. Wayne Duer was the only one who I can remember. He was like their leader. He was the first to stop dead, just looking at me, the other boys still game to have a go. I don't know why but at that moment, it was as if Wayne understood me. He sort of nodded his head at me. He called off his mates and away they went, one of them shouting back at me, "Fuckin homo!"

I was hardly gay. I was on my way to Lisa Hazeldine's house on Rose Crescent. She said that she'd only go out with me if I shaved my Mohican off. There was no chance of that. She went out with me anyway. Katrina, the girl who I mentioned earlier, was my real girlfriend – as I said I had been seeing her on and off since I was six. I was now sort of playing the field, as young boys often do, but Katrina was my main girlfriend and everyone knew it.

Mum and Dad, seeing my behaviour get progressively worse, decided to arrange with our John that I would go and stay with him in London.

Mum told me, "That thing's getting cut off before you go" – meaning my Mohawk.

While Mum, Dad and John sorted out the arrangements for my move South, I did have one last great day as a punk. Sefton Park in Liverpool put on a punk rock afternoon. Dressed in our best, most anarchic clothes, Callum and I made our way into Liverpool City Centre. As we had a few hours spare we went to Probe Records. We didn't have any money to spend – even so, it was a great place to hang out and meet like-minded kids. There were all kinds in there: Mods, soulies, punks, skins. I was in the basement with Callum flicking through the LPs when a voice came from behind us.

"You fellas all right down here?"

I turned around and there he was, six foot and dressed like a girl in a long white shirt, baggy white trousers, his makeup like a super model's and ribbons and things tied in his hair. I shat myself. Everyone in the basement went quiet. A couple of Mods nodded their heads to him. He just laughed, turned away and made his way back up the couple of steps. This was before Pete Waterman got his hands on him. Dead or Alive were cool as fuck. Pete Burns was the first cross-dresser I ever saw.

Me and Callum made our way to Sefton Park and we spent the day up a tree drinking cider and smoking Embassy Regal one after the other. The day over, I had to go back home and face my mother's scissors.

The next morning, my bag packed, I sat with Buster in the kitchen and waited for our Mick's mate, Les Martin, to come and collect me. He was going to his mother's house in Hemel Hempstead in Hertfordshire so had agreed to give me a lift down South. Our Mick gave him the use of his Austin Mini, it wasn't a 1275 gt but it was rapid. Mum and Dad gave me £25 and told me to behave myself when I got to London. I could see that my mum was upset but, really, I think that my parents were just glad that I was getting out of Skem.

Les came and got me. We had to first make a stop at Bagir Clothing Company to see John Deegan, the security guard. Les parked the car across the street and got out to talk to John. Big mistake because he had left the engine running. I climbed into the driver's seat, put the car into first gear and took off screaming on to the main road. I crashed the car up the kerb and through the bushes, coming to rest inches from the security fence. I was in shock. I just sat there. The engine was revving so loud. Les came running over, put his hand through the open window and turned the engine off.

"Paul, what the fuck are you doing? Are you trying to fuckin kill yourself?"

I can still see the look of horror on their faces as I killed Mick's Mini. Les climbed in and he reversed the car out of the bushes. I started laughing because the car had only gone a few feet. It was wobbling all over the place.

I turned to Les and said, "Do you think it will make it to London?"

"You're having a fuckin laugh aren't you? It's like something out of Billy Smart's fuckin Circus."

We dumped the car around the corner. We made our way into Liverpool and took the train to London Euston. This is one of the moments when our Mick really did want to strangle the life out of me. That's how I departed Skelmersdale. Mum and Dad were right to get me out of there.

I had no choice but to grow up fast once I was inducted into our John's kitchen. Three hundred knives, forks, spoons, plates, cups, saucers – you name it – I was washing it. Then came the pots and pans. Even though the kitchen was madly busy and sometimes chaotic, I loved it. John had given me a new direction and I had no longing to return home, other than for Katrina.

I wrote to her and occasionally I called but we soon drifted apart. I went back from time to time to see her. We were still as close as ever. I asked her to come and live in London. She said that her mum and dad wouldn't let her.

A few weeks later she then moved to Jersey with her new boyfriend. Not long after that, they invited me to their engagement party. I was gutted, but as usual the ability to cover up my feelings kicked in – and the clown inside me who accepts the destruction of everything that means anything to him took over. I accepted the situation and, after their little shindig, I went back to London. Another failed relationship. I'm still only sixteen and even though I was having fun in London, and I was surrounded by all these new people, I was still very confused and totally unsure of my identity. I really didn't know where I fitted in, in all of this.

John had lots of young chefs in his kitchen who went to college and earned their positions in his kitchen. Wanting to see me get on, he spoke to the greengrocer who delivered in Berkshire about a trainee chef's job that was up for grabs at the Horswell Estate in Ascot. An interview was arranged and a few days later I got the job. I was overjoyed, sixteen and out on my own.

The Horswell Estate was a training ground for polo ponies and also had a bronze foundry making figurines of racehorses, foxes, that sort of thing. About fifteen young people worked there, and there were also lots of young people coming and going due to the horse interest.

I made friends quickly – and I had relevant experience.

When I was about eleven, I was given the task of looking after a pony called Topper, a Welsh Mountain who lived on Holland's Farm not far from Skelmersdale. So riding and taking care of a horse was no problem.

The Farm Manager, B, asked me if I wanted to look after a horse called Captain. He had lost his left eye during a polo match, so he was a bit neglected. When we went out at five-thirty in the morning, the young grooms who lived on the estate would give me a bit of stick but I didn't care. Captain, as far as I was concerned, was my horse and I started taking him out in the afternoon, too.

The grounds of the estate went on for miles. Captain and I would take off in one direction and then I would lay in the long grass and fall asleep while he did his horse thing. It was either this or he would be locked in his stable all day.

The next thing, B came into the kitchen and said, "We're getting rid of Captain. He's going to another farm."

Bullshit, they put him down because the estate was cutting back financially. Gutted yet again, I protested that I would have taken care of him. It was no use. He was already dead.

I didn't want to stick around after that, so I applied for a job in Watford – the Shoux Shop Bakery in Bushey where I met a group of students. They were all into smoking pot and taking speed and acid. We had some wild parties. They had a couple of electric guitars, so I bought a small drum kit off my then boss, Steve. Here I go again, in the mood for music. We were terrible. We couldn't even play *Pretty Vacant* by the Sex

Pistols. Every time we got into a rhythm one of us would start giggling.

It was great fun in Watford. I invited a load of lads and girls from Skem down for a party. They didn't want to leave, and that was my cue to get out of there.

In 1988, John was now Head Chef at the Bear and Ragged Staff in Cumnor Village just outside Oxford. He again gave me a position in his kitchen, only this time I wasn't washing dishes. Here is John's interview technique:

"Right bollocks, this is your section of the kitchen. Keep it clean and tidy. With regards to the food, if in doubt, throw it out."

"Yer, but John, what am I doing exactly?"

"What you're fucking told."

That was it. I settled in quickly. One day I was out the back of the kitchen and what I can only describe as an angel walked past me. Jane was absolutely stunning. Blonde hair, big blue eyes, petite and sexy. God she was gorgeous. She walked past as if to get into her car, she then turned and walked back into the kitchen.

"Are you Paul?" She asked.

"Err, yer."

"Oh, your John said that you could make me a cake for my friend's birthday."

We talked cake for a minute and then she left. I felt compelled to follow her. As I walked out to the car park, I had already made my mind up to ask her out. Jane was fumbling by the side of her car. I asked her out immediately. She replied with, "Oh my god, I was just going to come in and ask you the same question." We fell madly in love.

It wasn't long before that self-destructive shitbag that lives inside of me reared his ugly head. I ended the relationship just before Christmas in 1989. To this day, I have no explanation as to why I hurt her. It took me years to understand just how much I really hurt myself. Breaking up with Jane only added to the emotional baggage that I was already laden with.

This was the best time of my life and I fucked it up. "*I see myself as an intelligent, sensitive human being with the soul of a clown which always forces me to blow it at the most crucial moments,*" Jim Morrison, The Doors.

I had to leave the Bear and Ragged Staff after what I did to Jane. I had really hurt her. I got a transfer within the company I worked for, a few miles further down the A420 towards Swindon. The Lamb and Flag at Southmoor Village wasn't much of a restaurant at the time but it was my first kitchen, so I was quite proud of myself. I was only there a couple of weeks and I had already made advances towards one of the waitresses, Jackie. Blonde, blue eyes, petite… starting to see a pattern? I guess I was pining for Jane right from the start.

A new management couple came into The Lamb and Flag. I was just getting settled there and now this pair of Herberts have come in wanting to change menus and God knows what. There was no reason to change a thing. We were doing over three hundred meals a week. I told the barman what I thought of them and their ideas. The little shit passed on what I had said, in the hope of saving his own job. The next morning, the manager came into the kitchen and asked me if it was true.

"Yes, it is, and I'm leaving on Friday."

His response: "Well, can I have that in writing?"

The truth was, I had nowhere to go. I had to get out and start looking for a job. I drove around the countryside from village to village. At the time, there were lots of restaurants and bars opening so I was confident that I would land something soon. After a couple of days, I again found myself a little further down the A420 in the direction of Swindon. On the left I noticed a sign, 'The Lamb Inn, next right'. As I made my way into the village, I noticed a large thatched cottage, the kind you see on chocolate boxes or a Christmas card full of snow.

At the time I didn't know it but one of its occupants, Sasha, would be in my life for the next twelve years.

I continued further into the village and there it was: The Lamb Inn, Bar, Restaurant, newly refurbished and built with the finest Cotswold stone. I parked the car and made my way over to some double glass doors that led onto the patio. As I got closer, a blonde lady moved quickly across the bar and snibbed on the lock.

"Can I help you?" she asked, fluttering her eyelashes.

I introduced myself and went on to tell her that I was looking for a job.

"Oh, you will have to speak with my husband Michael about that. He'll be here around eight, call back then."

I was so happy inside that I skipped up the steps back to my car.

Seven forty-five and I am back at The Lamb. I stepped through the patio doors. There were two men propping up the bar and an older gentleman sitting to the right. I noticed that his hands were shaking, and he was drinking through a straw. I asked the guys at the bar if one of them was Michael. They all found this rather amusing, and from behind the bar came this six-foot fellow who bellowed, "I am Michael. What the bloody hell do you want?"

I began to reel off my employment history as fast as I could, explaining that I was a chef looking for a job.

"Sod all that," he says. "Can you pull a pint?"

"Er – yeah."

"Well get behind the bar. Three bitters and a whisky for Mr Brighton. Don't forget his straw."

That was it, I was the new barman and waiter – just like that. I would later find out that that's how Michael was with everyone who wanted to work for him. Either you can do your job, or you can bloody well sod off. Great man.

When Lois, the Manager, had his days off, I would fill in for him and when Dave the chef was off, I was in the kitchen.

Behind the bar was where I really wanted to be. I loved chatting to the locals. Coming from a council estate in Skelmersdale, to me these people were top notch – the kind of people who I used to stare in at through double-glazed windows on the posh estate back home. I was amazed how quickly they took to me, and me to them. I would tell them wild stories about what I got up to as a kid.

They were mostly intrigued to know how on earth I ended up in Buckland. When I first met one of the older ladies of the village, Vivian, I told her that I was from an estate in Lancashire, to which Vivian asked in her ever-so-posh voice:

"Paul, what is your family name?"

To which, I replied, "McCarthy."

"No, no, I don't think I know that name. Is it a common name?" she asked.

I couldn't control myself. I burst out laughing and said, "Of course it is Vivian; I'm from a council estate, not a posh one."

"Har-har-har!" Vivian thought that this was hilarious. Even her laugh was posh.

That's how it was all the time. I loved telling them stories and after a few too many drinks some of them were all too happy to dish the dirt.

For a short time after leaving The Lamb and Flag, our John let me stay at his house in Abingdon. It was a bit of a drive to and from Buckland, so I decided to stick around during the day, getting the bar and the restaurant ready for the evening.

Vivian, who was now becoming a good friend and drinking companion, quickly understood that going to and from our John's house was getting a bit too much – I had told her how he preferred his privacy over his brother. Vivian suggested that I move into her house. She had a small room, annexed off from the rest of her home. I accepted her offer immediately.

"You can have the small room Paul, for £30 a week. I don't want anyone in the house and no loud music."

Vivian was lovely. She smoked like a chimney – and she loved a good several bottles of wine – but despite the age difference, we hit it off instantly.

At this point in my life I was so happy. I had just got together with Sasha, who was working as a waitress at the Lamb, I had a great job and now a place to live in the village. And it wouldn't be long before I met Thom.

Charlie Wellesley came into the bar from time to time.

Charlie's great-great-grandfather was the famous Duke of Wellington after he had kicked the living bejesus out of the French. The Duke had lived at Buckland House, a huge mansion just up the hill from the village. The house had long been closed but the grounds were kept in good order. I asked Charlie whether it would be okay if I walked in the grounds one afternoon.

"Of course, Paul. Just don't go too close to the house."

Spring was in the air. I felt great. I would close up the bar and go for a wander around the village. Buckland really is a fantastic place; everywhere you look is a picture postcard. On my travels I would often bump into the locals going about their daily routine. However, one person persisted on antagonising me, even though I did nothing to deserve his attention. He just kept on at me: Martin 'Miss Marple' Holder, the village policeman. Right from the start he went out of his way to harass me. What a terrible excuse for law enforcement he turned out to be.

All the villagers had the utmost respect for Martin. He represented The Law and I had no problem with that. Even though my dad had a few run-ins with the police, he still respected them for the job that they had to do, and he often told me how shit the world would be without them.

Of course he was right, but growing up in a town full of Scousers we all grew to hate the police. They were bullies and liars back then. In the 70s and 80s they still had that air of untouchability. The local copper could give a kid a good hiding and some of the parents would thank him for keeping their kids in check – can you imagine that today?

When I was a kid, I had seen my father with a broken arm and a bashed-in face, the local coppers did that to him. I can remember them pushing my mum down the stairs to get at him. No such thing as a search warrant back then.

It turned out that the stupid sods were at the wrong house; they were after John Ahern who lived two doors away.

I always said calling them pigs was an insult to a bacon butty.

To me, Martin was just another bully in a hat and I had no problem letting him know exactly how I felt. It wasn't long before he would prove me right – and on more than one occasion.

Walking the grounds of Buckland House, I found myself reciting poetry that I had written as a teenager. I quickly realised that my passion for verse was still alive and well. What can I say? I was inspired.

I went back to the bar, fixed myself a drink, grabbed a pen and paper and went outside and sat on the patio. I began to write a few lines, nothing I could really get to grips with. Then, I noticed in one of the flowerbeds a blackbird doing its best to eat a large black beetle. They were just a feet away from me yet the blackbird showed no fear whatsoever. The beetle on the other hand knew exactly what was in store. It was truly fighting for its life. I sat quietly watching until the blackbird beat up the beetle, just enough to swallow it.

The Blackbird
The bird, it stalks, just as the beast,
watching in anticipation for the success
of this forthcoming meal.

The pose is adopted, and the stance
is cast, its eyes transfixed
to the tiny creature's movements.

Aha – the crunch of the small
dark suit of armour and the creature
passes forth, to the oncoming dimension.

No sounds of pain, no sounds of glory,
yet the Blackbird will continue
as an ever-advancing army

I was beside myself; I couldn't believe that after all this time I'd come up with that.

From that moment on I was writing, and every available minute was spent in the grounds of Buckland House. I would sit under one of the large trees on the approach for hours and write stories of explanation, poetry, lyrics, songs – even nonsense. I would focus on just one word and WHAM – just like that another masterpiece. Well, they were to me.

The patio at The Lamb, where I wrote *The Blackbird* and many more poems. Behind those double doors is where Thom and I shared our dreams. It all began in that bar. It has changed inside now but, when I visited to take these photos, it felt like I had never left. I think that's down to my unwillingness to forgive and forget. The two windows upper left are from the apartment I had above the restaurant. Thom and I had some great times up there, stoned off our heads watching black-and-white Charlie Chaplin movies.

Soon I was reciting my poetry to Vivian. Many an afternoon I would lock the front door and we would sit in front of the open fire. As long as Vivian had her fags and a glass of wine, she was not moving for anyone. Vivian loved my poetry and she encouraged me to keep it up.

One summer afternoon she took me into Oxford to meet one of her lawn-tennis-playing friends who also happened to be an English tutor. He did his best to induct me into one of his classes, but it wasn't to be. We ended up as drunk as skunks on Little Clarendon Street.

One day, Vivian came to The Lamb with a friend. We sat together for most of the afternoon, and then Vivian suggested that I read my poetry to them. By now I had notebooks filled with the stuff. Just another fine day at The Lamb. Vivian's friend Marie was much like her: beautiful to talk to and in real great shape for her age. She seemed really kind and fun to be around. We had a great day and after a few bottles of wine we said our goodbyes.

As they were about to leave, Marie turned to me and said, "Oh Paul, my son Edward is coming home for the weekend, shall I ask him to call in for a drink?"

"Yes of course," I replied.

The following Saturday I was a little late getting back from the brewery in Abingdon. As I walked into the bar; I noticed a tall chap standing next to a young blonde lady.

"Are you Paul?" he asked.

"Yes, I am," I said, as I made my way behind the bar.

"You spoke with my mother the other day."

"Oh, you must be Edward?"

"Er no, Ed. Just call me Ed, okay?"

"Yer but your name is Edward."

He replied, "My mum calls me Edward, but I hate it."

Odd, I thought, how you can hate your own name.

Edward and I got on quite well at first. I thought that he was a really nice lad, and after a couple of meetings with him, he asked if I'd like to go for drinks with him and a group of his friends in Oxford one Friday night. We arranged to meet at Browns Café where he was working part-time as a barman. I was really looking forward to going out with him. As I said, I thought that he was good company and a laugh to be around.

Friday night came and Lois let me leave work at 10pm. I took a taxi into Oxford and made my way to Browns. Edward was still working. He gave me a drink and I sat around for an hour waiting for him.

We made our way to a club called Downtown Manhattans. It was situated beneath an old bingo hall. I was really excited. I had never been clubbing as I had worked since I was fifteen, so I was looking forward to this night out. I felt a little anxious as I wasn't sure what to expect but, mostly, I was nervous inside. I put on a brave face and I got on with it.

The club wasn't busy. We made our way over to a group of boys and girls my own age. Edward didn't introduce me. I knew one of the lads there, he was a resident DJ at Raoul's Wine Bar on Walton Street. His name was Sean, so I said hello to him, and he then introduced me to the others. I got a drink and leant back against the bar doing my best to look as cool as possible in my tweed hunters jacket.

Edward was moving from one person to the next. It was as if he was walking in slow motion. Four boys and three girls, one after the other they looked directly at me. *I am obviously the gooseberry* is what I was thinking. As Edward got to Sean, he whispered in his ear and Sean reached into his pocket and pulled out a packet of chewing gum.

He stepped towards me and handed me one saying, "Here Paul have one of these. You have garlic breath."

I looked back at Edward who had now moved into the middle of the group of girls – the look of pity on all their faces, and Edward now looking ever so fucking pleased with himself.

I glared right at him. I realised now why he was sloping round like a fuckin snake. I couldn't believe what he had just done. Why not tell me himself? No one had ever made me feel like this and I am sure to this day he took great pride in belittling me in front of them.

The club was shit and now having the confidence kicked out of me, I said my goodbyes.

As I was about to leave, Edward calls from behind me, "Hey Paul, my friend Thom is coming back from uni this week, shall I ask him to call into The Lamb for a drink?"

"Yes okay, ask him to call me first," I replied.

As I made my way up the stairs to leave the club, I remember thinking, *Not if he's anything like you.*

I took a taxi back to Buckland. *Never again*, I thought.

A few days later I had forgotten all about Edward and his sloping snake incident. I was busy in the bar getting the place ready for the evening. It was March, and the weather was becoming worse by the day. The wind was blowing quite bad, making the front door open slightly then bang shut. It was getting on my nerves, but I wanted to get the bar ready before I closed up for a few hours. The phone rings around 3.15pm.

"Hello is that Paul? It's Thom, I'm a friend of Edward's."

We arranged that he'd call round for a drink about 4.30pm. The front door was still banging open and shut so I didn't notice him as he came in. I looked up and there he was, dressed in a dark-grey overcoat four or five times too big for him, a pair of old faded blue jeans – also four or five times too big – a large black leather belt pulled tight around his waist to gather up the loose denim, a blue tie-dye T-Shirt and a pair of hobnailed boots (also way too big for him and without doubt they had not seen a brush of polish in years). His head was shaved and he had a few days' growth on his face.

Thom put out his arms and turned his palms to face me. He tilted his head to one side, as if to say, 'This is it'. He truly was a pathetic sight.

I walked from behind the bar and shook his hand.

"Come and sit at the bar, Thom. I'm almost finished here."

He sat on a stool just in front of me. I asked him what he would like to drink and with that he pulled out a handful of 1p, 2p and 5p coins. He spread them on the bar and said, "Is this enough for a half? It's all the money that I have."

I looked at the coins, and then back at him.

"Well, is it?" he said.

We both started laughing.

"Fuck me, Thom. That's not even enough for a quarter!"

We sat there giggling. That was it – instant friends.

After that first meeting, we were always together and, from that moment on, he knew that he never had to pay for a thing.

We spent that first week smoking pot, drinking till late in the bar, talking for hours about music and life, getting to know one another. Every night I would have a packet of Silk Cut cigarettes and, when he was leaving, whatever was left in the packet I would give him, along with a small lump of hash.

The following Sunday he said he would be leaving in the morning to make his way back to Exeter. I bought him two packs of Silk Cut from the cigarette machine, then I went to the till in the bar and took out thirty quid. I handed it to him as he was leaving. He was gobsmacked.

"Shit Paul, are you sure?"

"Of course, Thom, just take it."

"I'll pay you back Paul. I promise."

I told him that I didn't want anything back.

As he turned to leave, he said, "Paul, I usually stay in Exeter at –" I stopped him.

"Sound Thom. See you when you get back." He just sniggered to himself and left.

The next few months with Thom were a non-stop laugh. He got to know Sasha and everyone at The Lamb really quickly. We were the only people for miles, so everyone soon became friends.

Christmas was around the corner. I asked Michael if I could give Thom a job in the kitchen, helping Dave.

Michael being the ever-sharp business man said, "Yes Paul, he can work over the holidays but as he is your friend, you can pay his wages."

Five pounds fifty pence an hour and Thom had a job throughout Christmas 1990.

We had a great Christmas. I did buy him a present but for the life of me I can't remember what it was. Maybe it was hash and that's why I can't remember.

The holidays over, Thom made his way back to uni. Over the next few weeks I didn't see him much as he was cracking on with his degree. I often went over to Abingdon for a night out with our John. We would sit in the Feathers Pub and get plastered, walk back to his house knocking one another about like drunken louts.

When I woke up at John's one morning, I looked out of his spare bedroom window and it was totally white out. I made my way downstairs. John had already left for work.

His wife seeing the look on my face asked, "You ok Paul?"

"No, not really. I haven't driven in snow before."

"Oh, don't worry," she said. "You'll be all right."

I had only been driving for a year and that was mostly thanks to Jane and her mother for allowing me to have driving lessons in their car.

As I made my way through Marcham village on the A315, the snow was even worse. I skidded into the back of a broken-down Sherpa Van. I was then hit from behind by a young lad in a Ford Sierra. My Fiat X19 now pretty bashed up, I made my way back to John's house. I telephoned Michael at The Lamb, and I made my excuses. I put my car in John's garage and I took a taxi to work the next morning.

When I arrived Michael and his wife Pam were waiting for me. Pam was really excited to tell me how I had missed a great night at The Lamb. She explained that the electricity had gone out all over the village as the snow had brought down the power cables. Lots of locals had made their way to The Lamb to seek some kind of shelter – "we had candles everywhere!"

Apparently, Fred the farmer brought his friends who were in a skiffle band, and as the gas supply was still on, Pam made food for everyone in the bar, free of charge.

Michael then tells me, "Your mate Thom turned up looking for you. We know that he has no money Paul but, don't worry, we took good care of him. He helped out by collecting glasses and serving drinks and the girls made sure that he had plenty of drinks. He was well looked after."

When Michael referred to the girls, he meant his two daughters. They were both really kind and lovely. The youngest of them, just twelve, still sucked her thumb. She was still a giggling little girl. She absolutely wouldn't harm a fly.

My Iron Lung, off the album *The Bends* – when I first understood the contents of this song, years later, I tell you, I really did want to give Thom that kick up the arse he once so desired.

> *Suck, suck your teenage thumb*
> *Toilet trained and dumb*
> *When the power runs out, we'll just hum*
> *This, this is our new song*
> *Just like the last one*
> *A total waste of time*
> *My iron lung*

As you know, an iron lung helps you to breathe. The way I see it is, I was the one who helped Thom to breathe, so in a sense I was his iron lung.

I swear, I was really pissed off when I heard this song. Here is Thom accepting the kindness from the people in my life, they took him in, this is his thank-you.

"You know what? Your skiffle band is shit and your daughter is a fucking idiot!"

He might as well have said it, just like that. These people may never hear any of Radiohead's songs. Does that make it all right? Not in my book.

During my research prior to writing this memoir, I was safe in the knowledge that Thom, as far as I was aware, had not used any content from *The Blackbird*. I still believe that to be the case, but if you are familiar with the video to the track *There, There*, from the album *Hail to the Thief*, the visual references are there. At the end of the video, Thom morphs into a tree trunk. Only his face remains, a permanent reminder for all to see.

When I first became aware of the video's contents, I have to tell you, I was a little freaked out. Out in the car park of The Lamb Inn, there are three massive conker trees. One Saturday afternoon, I was sitting in the bar with Thom and some tree surgeons turned up to cut the conker trees back. What I thought was going to be a quick job turned into a two-day affair. By the time the guys had finished stripping off the branches, all that was left were three trunks as bald as they could be. They looked more like three poorly attempted totem poles.

They were still standing about ten metres tall, straight up, and Thom and I joked how they looked more like fingers sticking up from the ground. I suggested that we cut down the left and right tree trunk to halfway to give the impression of someone sticking up their middle finger. Anyway, until we got bored this seemed an amusing focal point.

The next weekend, I was with Sasha in the bar. The pub was quiet mid-afternoon so I suggested going outside to take some photographs of her. She was stunning to look at, so it made sense. We made our way over to the now balding conker trees. At the bottom of them, the tree surgeons had left a collection of logs, all different lengths and widths. Sasha sat and posed for a few pictures. I then ran to the bar and came back with a small kitchen knife. Just head height, I carved a love heart and, in the middle, I carved our names and the date, declaring our existence.

I will always be part of the history at The Lamb Inn, as long as 'the three fingers' remain standing.

During the video for the track *There there (The Bony King of Nowhere)*, there were several references to this moment along with a few pointers to the poem, *The Blackbird*. Thom is pursued through the woods by blackbirds. His feet rise into the air as he tries to escape, his hands flapping wildly at his sides, giving him lift.

This is not his nightmare, it is mine.

I told Thom about this recurring dream I'd had for years – even now I still have it. I am being pursued by God knows what or who. I lean back as I am running away and as I flap my hands by my sides, my feet rise from the ground, so that I am flying feet first.

We sat in the bar one night talking about this dream. I leaned backwards on some chairs showing him the hand-flapping motion while I lifted my feet off the ground. We even went as far as obtaining a dream book off Vivian so that we could find out its meaning, if any.

Now, in this video, Thom's flying feet first until finally, in the last few frames, he metamorphoses into the third tree – the three trees a direct reference to the trees that stand to this day in the car park at The Lamb Inn in Buckland village. Before, when I said that I was a little freaked out by this, I wasn't joking. I spent months pondering what he could possibly mean or gain by using this imagery. I would spend hours going over things in my mind. What does he want? Is he sending me a message? I conveyed this to Sasha, and she thought it best that I go around and, as she put it, "punch his lights out".

Can you imagine what this – plus all the other nonsense combined over the years – was doing to my mind? It just got more and more unbearable to deal with.

Well, Radiohead fans: say hello to the tree fingers. I told you about the fun that Thom and I had taking the mickey out of the tree surgeons' handy work. As you can see, there are three trees just like in the video for the track *There there* – and if you look at the prior picture you will see where I carved my name in the bark. In the video, Thom morphs into the third tree trunk as if for all eternity. Honestly, I was fucking freaked out for years over this. Can you imagine trying to explain it to someone when you're out of your nut all the time? Thank fuck I'm straight now.

Edward had not been around at all since our last unfortunate outing. I thought that everyone had gone back to uni but he and his girlfriend were still around. They came into the bar just after New Year and, after a couple of drinks, Edward and I start talking about Oliver Stone's forthcoming movie, *The Doors*. I wanted to make a big deal about the whole thing and get everyone dressed up in 60s clothes for the opening night and really go for it. Just like that he then says, "Yer, I'm in a band, and Thom is the singer."

I swear I nearly choked on my apple juice.

"Thom hasn't said anything about a band."

"No Paul, he's really uncomfortable discussing it with anyone."

I couldn't believe what I was hearing – the nights that Thom and I had spent talking about music and how I was really disappointed that I never followed my dreams of becoming a poet, a rock star or even an actor. I told Thom many times that one of my goals in life was to have my name on a record. That's very easy by today's standards, but back then, making records was still a thing for major labels and the select few. All these months and Thom had said nothing. I asked Edward if they had any songs recorded. He told me that they had a three-track demo.

"Paul," he said. "I don't think that Thom will play it to you. He's really unsure about it."

My mind now racing, I couldn't wait to see Thom. I was buzzing inside.

I made my way back to Vivian's that afternoon, but I couldn't stop thinking about Thom and the band. I went back to the bar and called Thom at uni – I couldn't get hold of him. Thankfully, later that evening he called back and I told him about the conversation that I'd had with Edward. I asked him why he hadn't told me about his band. He didn't want to talk about it.

"I'll be back at the weekend Paul. I'll talk to you then."

Well the next few days could not have gone any slower. I kept thinking about this demo and what its contents could be. I had no idea what they sounded like or what kind of music they played, but in my mind I had already made the decision that I wanted to get involved. In which capacity, I didn't yet know.

Finally, Thom arrived at the bar and straight away we again went on and on about music. Only this time we spoke about him and his band. I asked him again why he hadn't told me about it.

He just shrugged his shoulders and said, "I don't know Paul. I just don't think that anyone will like it."

I asked him if I could listen to the demo. He was adamant that I wouldn't like it and, at first, he refused – but after continuously badgering him I think he agreed just to shut me up.

The next afternoon, Thom turned up at the bar. He looked petrified. I asked him if he had brought the demo.

"Yes Paul, but you can have it when I leave. I don't want you to play it while I'm here."

I asked him why he was so afraid to let me play it right then. He became so uncomfortable that I backed off and we had a lengthy conversation about confidence. I told him that it didn't matter if anyone likes it.

I said, "Listen Thom, you're in a band. You've made some records. Even if they are shit, who cares? Just be proud of the fact that you're doing it. Do you know what I'd give to be in a band right now and I am not the only person who feels like this. For fuck's sake Thom, at least you're halfway there."

I knew that I was getting through to him. I could see it in his eyes. He was ever so timid when we first met and after talking to him the way that I did, I could see the strength building within him. He would analyse everything that I said to him. This wasn't confined to conversations about music. We discussed everything: parents, school, bullies, girls, the way he looked.

Confidence, confidence and more confidence. I told him how when I get nervous, I approach things with a certain amount of anger inside me. "Be aggressive," I told him, "but remain kind and understanding". I would force the issue with him, whatever it may be. I did on occasion make him angry, I know, but that helped him to say, "Fuck it", and he got on with things. We had a conversation about Karen Carpenter and how she had starved herself to death because she believed that she was fat. I pointed out how ridiculous that was and how much of our own despair is in our minds.

"Who gives a fuck what you look like?" I said.

Thom had never met anyone like me. He told me himself how he had never had anyone speak to him the way that I did. This is why we became so close. He knew that I wasn't going to bullshit him or mollycoddle him in any way.

I would say things to him like, "Pull yer fuckin socks up."

Just my Scouse accent was enough to make him laugh. Yet at the same time he knew full well what I meant.

Thom got up to leave, as he did, he handed me the demo.

"Please be careful with it Paul. It's the only copy we have."

Well for the first time, I couldn't wait for him to go – I almost threw him out of the bar. I waited until he passed by the window and, after waving him goodbye, I made my way over to the tape deck, took out the Bob Dylan cassette and set Thom's to play. I turned it up as loud as I could, and I made my way to the centre of the bar so that I could listen through all four speakers.

How am I going to convey what I felt when I first heard, *Stop Whispering*? This version was slightly different to the one on *Pablo Honey*. During the demo version, one of Thom's uni friends is rapping towards the end. Personally, I think that this track was much better than the one on the album. Anyway, here goes. I was nervous but excited to the max – I must have had a look of anticipation on my face like a four-year-old going to Disney Land. The track started and I realised that the stupid childish grin on my face had been replaced with something like the look of a teenager who had just had his first sexual encounter.

My mind was blown – the rise of the guitars, the peaking of the instruments that brings you crashing back to earth. Thom's voice. Oh my God, Thom's voice. I was fucking astounded that Thom, this quiet, tiny little thing, could be capable of such a powerful, head-exploding sound. I swear, I was instantly star struck, and I know that what I've just said doesn't really convey the experience that I had when I first played the tape.

This is the moment that I became Radiohead's first-ever true fan. To this day, I stand by that statement and no one, not anyone, can take this away from me. You Radiohead purists must be seething with jealousy and hatred by now.

After listening to the cassette repeatedly for about an hour, I took it back to Vivian's where I played it on my Walkman, over and over for the rest of the day.

I went back that evening and finished my shift in the bar. I had already made my mind up; I was going to ask Thom if I could promote the band. I really believed that I could do it. With my love for music and my friendship with him, I was sure that he would say yes. I went back to Vivian's that night and I played the cassette over and over until I went to sleep.

Thom turned up at The Lamb the next afternoon. I couldn't wait to see him, and as soon as he came into the bar, I was all over him.

"Thom, you have to let me promote you. I can't believe that this is you singing. Why didn't you tell me before? I could have started promoting you ages ago. Can I promote the band, Thom? I can do it, I swear. I have all the time in the afternoons, and I am off on Mondays so I can do the groundwork..."

On and on I went. I am sure that he only agreed to talk with the others just to shut me up.

He couldn't believe my reaction. He sat across the bar from me, listening as I went on about all the garbage that was getting played on the radio on a daily basis. Thom's band was by far in a better class. Even before Thom had the chance to tell the others about my request, we sat for days making the arrangements. I pushed and pushed him for answers as to where he wanted to go with this. He had no idea at this point, but the more I spoke about how great he and his sound were, the more the look of trepidation on his face slowly began to change into nervous excitement. It took a good few days to convince him how great he was.

"Paul, no one is committed. We are all over the place at the moment."

"So you need a bit of encouragement. Someone to help get things moving."

"Yes, that's exactly what we need."

Thom's biggest concern was his father. He knew that it would cause problems if he focused his energies on his music rather than on his degree. His studies came first, and Thom had made a point of letting me know that, right from the start.

Having convinced Thom of my ability to support and promote the band, he went back to uni promising me that he would talk with the others, and would get back to me as soon as he had an answer.

I had by now made friends with lots of people my own age who were coming and going, to and from uni.

Nyle was a handsome sod, six foot tall, blonde and naturally fit. His sister Mara was absolutely stunning to look at. They came to the bar every time they were back in the village.

Nyle's 21st birthday was around the corner – a black-tie affair to be held at the poshest hotel in central Oxford. I received my invite. A proper one. I had to RSVP for the first time in my life. When I sent it back, Nyle came to the bar to tell me that his mother was a little angry that he had invited me. As he put it:

"She thinks that you're a bit rough."

"What the fuck Nyle? Don't you mean that I'm too common."

"Yes Paul, something like that."

That was it. I told him that I wasn't going. I had only met his mother on one occasion, when I went into Oxford to have a drink with Nyle. I was upset that, from a two-minute meeting, she had taken an instant dislike to me. Too common. *Fuckin snob,* I thought.

"Forget it Nyle, I'm not going."

Nyle insisted on speaking to her. A couple of days later he came back to the bar and told me that she had relented and said that I could come but I was not allowed at any tables with other family members. This to my mind was more of an insult.

"Fuck that Nyle. What am I? A fuckin leper?"

He thought that this was funny, but I didn't. I was adamant that I wasn't going. Well after a couple of drinks, he convinced me to take no notice of her.

"I want you at my party Paul, and so does Mara."

He went on to tell me that loads of Mara's friends would be there.

My decision changed, I had to make a good impression. Nyle was studying Advertising. I went into Oxford and I bought his birthday gift – the most in-depth and expensive book that I could find relating to all aspects of advertising. Moss Bros was on the high street. I ordered the best tuxedo that they had for rent. I had to go back a couple of days later for a fitting. Across the road from Moss Bros was The Covered Market. I took Nyle's birthday gift into one of the little craft shops and I had one of the young ladies wrap it for me. It looked great. Vivian's friend Diana came to the house and she spent two hours doing my hair, Vivian's treat.

I turned up at the party looking like 007, gift in hand. The usher on the door looked at me with those eyes that said, "Shit, he's got a few bob". I walked through the large wooden doors into the massive party room. Black ties and ball gowns wall to wall. Nyle came straight over to me. I gave him his gift, then he took me to a table off to the left. Mara made a fuss telling me how fantastic I looked. I sat at the table with her uni friends. I glanced over and Nyle was standing next to his mother, showing off the gift that I had brought him. I made eye contact but she didn't acknowledge me.

I then noticed that the guy sitting with her was a friend of my doctor who I had known for about two years. He was a leading plastic surgeon, and he was also a regular at the Bear and Ragged Staff. He seemed so pleased to see me and immediately called me over. Now I don't know if it was the James Bond outfit or if the good doctor fought in my corner, but Nyle's mother apologised to me, saying that she was sorry for her rash judgement.

Myxomatosis is a poem that I wrote about a young rabbit I found in the Croft the day after Nyle's party. His mother had invited me to their house for afternoon tea – I suppose in some way to say sorry. When I got there, a few of Mara's friends had obviously stayed the night and were sitting around. One of these girls and I had hit it off the night before, so while we are having tea it became apparent to everyone there was a bit of a spark between us. Nyle's mother suggested that we go for a stroll around the village. It was a beautiful sunny day. The main group was up ahead. Myself and this young lady slowed right down, to everyone's amusement. We were just talking, enjoying one another's company. In the hedge that surrounded the Croft, we then heard a rustling sound. We looked and there was a baby rabbit, its eyes full of slime. It tried to run away from us, but it couldn't see a thing. Me doing my best to show Mara's friend my softer side, I jumped over the fence to catch the rabbit in my jacket and take it back to Vivian's.

There was no doubt that the rabbit had myxomatosis. Even so, I told the young lady that I would take good care of it. I put it in a box, and we made our way back to Nyle's.

Over the next few days, I bathed the rabbit's eyes in warm milk and I kept it well fed. Vivian had a black cat, and it knew full well that I had something in my room. Every morning it would be at my door waiting to get in.

The night that I told Thom about the rabbit, we sat in the bar with Sasha and got smashed. The next morning, when I woke up to go to the bathroom and opened my bedroom door, there was the cat, looking up at me with an ever-so-pleased look on its face. I brushed it aside and took one step into the hall. That's when I felt the cold sticky ooze under my right foot.

"What the..."

I looked down and the cat had chewed up and spread ooze right across my path. Bits of mouse all over the place.

When I told Thom and Michael about the rabbit, they said that I was crazy to waste my time and that I should have put it back where I found it and let nature take its course.

> *The mongrel cat came home*
> *Clutching half a head,*
> *Proceeded to show it off*

From *Myxomatosis*, track 12 off the album *Hail to the Thief*. I wrote my version a couple of days after finding the rabbit, along with another poem called *Mongrel Cat*. Noel Gallagher once went on about how fantastic it was to hear your songs being sung back to you, something you had created, that now had so much meaning to others. He said how amazing and proud he felt when the band would get it, and after just a few chords there was his song being played back to him. I related to this but, for me, there was no feeling of joy. I was up the side of a mountain in Spain packing a load of you-know-what into the arse-end of a truck, *Myxomatosis* now consuming me.

It's funny how something like this affects you. Although I was angry and confused, I still felt proud. That's my stuff on that record, despite the fact that, other than Radiohead, I was the only person on the planet who knew the origins of tracks like *Myxomatosis*. It was a very strange feeling indeed.

When I read *Myxomatosis* to Thom for the first time, he looked up at me, his face a combination of anger and disappointment.

"Is this about me?" he asked, convinced that I had written about his wonky eye.

When Thom rearranged the song, he says towards the

end *"No one likes a smart arse"*. Even though I'd explained to him that my poem was about the rabbit, that comment did my head in a little because I would never have said anything negative to him, or about him – I never did. There was not a chance that I would take the piss out of him in a poem. *No one likes a smart arse*; he got that wrong.

Vivian's House, where I lived with her and her cat. I penned *Myxomatosis* and *Mongrel Cat* here. Sitting in front of the roaring fireplace was epic (Vivian would be drunk of course). My room was behind the window on the left, and behind that front door is where her cat had spread the dead mouse.

Thom was pushing me to enter the Oxford University Press annual Competition for Poetry. The winner's work would be printed in the OUP Magazine in the forthcoming year.

My handwriting is worse than a doctor's, so I asked Tanya Mills if she would type ten of my poems out nice and neatly. Tanya was a friend of one of Michael's daughters. She came to work with me through the summer of '91. A gorgeous young lady she was. We got on great.

Tanya, Thom and I sat in the bar and we went through my notebooks of poetry, deciding which ones I should send. *Where They End and We Begin*, *Myxomatosis* and *Street Spirit* were among the ten selected.

Tanya took them home that night and she typed them out for me.

Thom came in the next day with the competition details. I sent them off and I waited.

A week or so later I received a letter from the OUP secretary thanking me for my submission, but I was too late – the poet for that year had already been chosen.

I was a little gutted but, even so, for me to receive a letter from the OUP was an achievement in itself.

In the summer of 1990 Lois, the manager at The Lamb, decided to put on a Spanish day. Michael asked the local blacksmith to make a ten-foot frying pan and he rented six gas burners. The Old Barn across the car park was set out like a makeshift kitchen. By this time the chef Dave had left, so me and Lois shared the kitchen duties as well as the day-to-day running of the place. Lois invited his flamenco-playing guitarist friend to come and entertain everyone.

They made gallons upon gallons of sangria the day before, so they were well and truly sozzled that morning. I ran the day from start to finish. I organised the waitresses from the other restaurants that I had worked at, together with Sasha, and Thom again was in the kitchen washing dishes.

I made sure that each waitress had only two tables each to deal with and under no circumstances were they to leave them unattended. I knew how important these people were to Michael. I cooked the paella and the girls took it in turns to deliver the piping-hot food to their tables. The day went brilliantly. Everyone had a great time. By 8.30pm the bar was quiet. Sasha, Thom and I stayed on and got shit-faced. The next morning, I walked into the bar and Michael and Pam were there waiting for me.

I asked, "Where's Lois?"

Michael said, "He won't be coming back. Here are the keys to the place – do you want them?"

I didn't quite understand what was going on.

"What for?" I asked.

Pam then says, "Paul, we watched you all day yesterday. There's not much point Lois being here. His job is yours if you want it. Our daughter Bailey is moving out of the apartment upstairs. You can have that as well."

By this time my mouth is open and for the first time in my life I don't know what to say.

Michael then says, "We are also giving you an extra £100 a week." He dangles the keys in front of me and says, "Well, do you want them or not?"

Sasha, Thom, the band, my own apartment, the keys to the place, Manager. Now you would think that at twenty-four this would be my career mapped out in front of me. My life for the first time ever felt perfect. What could possibly go wrong?

Just getting back to Nyle's mother for a second, I do have to laugh. If she could see me now – sitting in my prison cell at HMP Swaleside, writing this, wearing nothing but my boxer shorts – I dread to think what she would have to say. I tell you this though, Nyle's mother was about the straightest, most honest person I came across in that village. At least she had the guts to say what she felt. Others I met in Buckland were three-faced, never mind, two-faced.

The guy who owned the newsagent's in Southmoor village came into the bar one day, asking me who I'd had over a few days before. I was a little confused by his line of questioning.

My brother John had come over to see me one afternoon. We had something to eat, a couple of drinks, and then he went back to Abingdon. This guy is now wanting to know who I had over.

"Why?" I asked him.

I swear, I couldn't believe the shit that came out of his mouth, and this is the God's honest truth:

"Well Paul, somebody smashed a kitchen window at old Mrs Moore's and stole two china dolls worth a lot of money. I found out yesterday that you had your friends here. Did they steal the dolls?"

I fuckin lost it. I opened the fire escape door, which never got opened other than for Mr Brighton. I said, "Listen here you stupid cunt, get the fuck out of this bar and don't ever come back."

"I'm only asking Paul," he said.

"Get the fuck out, go on, fuck off out of it."

I never saw him again at the bar. He made sure that this shit-faced rumour went around the village, and, as far as I'm concerned, this is the fuel that gave Thom the inspiration for *No Surprises*, track 10 on *OK Computer*.

> *Such a pretty house*
> *And such a pretty garden*
> *No alarms and no surprises*
> *(get me out of here)*

The old lady who was robbed was famous in the local area for her pretty house and well-kept flower beds – she had won competitions for her gardening. It was also reported that she had no security alarm.

People were coming into the bar asking what had gone on. A few weeks later the village bobby Martin Holder and his wife made an appearance in the bar, and what an appearance this turned out to be.

I was sitting with Thom and a young couple from Southmoor village. It was a quiet night, so we were in front of the open fire having a bit of a laugh.

Martin and his now witch-hunter wife walk in. I made my way behind the bar and I asked them what they would like to drink. As I turned my back on them to pour their drinks, Martin pipes up.

"Hey Paul, it's really irresponsible to take Sasha out in her mother's car."

His wife then jumps in.

"Yes Paul, Sasha is not insured for that car. If she had an accident, she would be in a lot of trouble."

I couldn't believe the bullshit that they were coming out with.

The previous week, Sasha's parents had gone on holiday, leaving her alone in the house. I had stayed there for a few days – but taking the car out? Not a chance. Sasha was shit-scared of her father, so as far as I was concerned, this verbal nonsense was yet another attempt by some twat in the village to make trouble for me.

A week or two before, I had bought a Sony Dictaphone.

It was easier to recite poetry and record it, rather than write it down. The Dictaphone was on the table by the open fire. Thom, on hearing the two witch hunters' accusations, sets the Dictaphone to record. He walks past me behind the bar, saying, "Can I get some ice?", then slips the Dictaphone in between me and my accusers. I got on to it straight away. I then pushed and pushed these two, so that they repeated their nonsense many times over.

The story of this recording went around the village like the plague. Everyone was talking about it. Martin, now realising that he has shit the bed, goes around to Michael's house and he pleaded with him to get the recording off me. When Michael came to the bar, he was upset that the police were at his door. What I couldn't understand was, why was he so upset with me? What the fuck did I do?

I told Michael that I had given the Dictaphone to Thom, which was the truth. I then told him that Thom had recorded over it because he didn't want any trouble. As far as I know, Thom might still have the Dictaphone, and its career-damaging contents. Just one last thing on this: have you guessed yet who told Martin I was with Sasha in the car? Yes, the stupid sod from the china doll incident – and from what I was told it was his wife that started the rumour. This will not be the first and only run-in I have with Martin 'Miss Marple' Holder. He and his wife had been made to look like fools and, from that moment on, he was out to get me.

Oliver Stone's movie *The Doors* was due for release. My love for Jim Morrison and the 60s – and now this movie – was all I could talk about. Many nights Thom and I discussed the 60s scene and how I would've loved to have been part of it – the clothes, the music, the flower power. I think that this is one of the reasons why Vivian and I got on so well. She was part of the 60s London scene.

I was born in 1967, the Summer of Love. I was connected to the 60s but I was obviously born a bit too late to enjoy them. I longed for that 60s vibe. Oliver Stone's movie would now be a window into the life of The Doors and – more importantly for me – I'd be able to get to know Jim Morrison. Sure, I had seen a lot of things on TV over the years and lots of things in magazines, but this is what I longed for. That scene when go to Andy Warhol's Factory was what I had envisioned, yet I had never experienced it. On reflection, years after watching the film, I was so happy to see that Oliver Stone hadn't, like so many, forgotten the gorgeous Miss Edie Sedgwick. Drugged up, forced out, but not forgotten.

My idea to go to the opening show in Oxford dressed in 60s clothes was now consuming me. I was adamant that I was going to try. I started growing my hair and I went to the Covered Market in Oxford and bought a load of different collared beads. The pictures of Jim Morrison taken by Patricia Kennealy wearing nothing more than his leather pants and a beaded necklace inspired me to make my own. I started making necklaces and bracelets for all my friends, Thom included. Mr Brighton's wife, seeing me sitting in the bar threading these things said, "Paul, I have some lovely beads at home, they are from the Island of Iona, in Scotland. You can't find them anywhere else on the planet. They're semi-precious. I will bring them for you next time I'm here."

A few days later, and sure enough Mrs Brighton gave me a small bag of these lovely yellowish-green stones. They had already been drilled ready for construction into whatever.

Thom was back at uni. I took the stones into Oxford and made my way to the craft shop in the Covered Market. With the help of the girls in the shop, we picked out a selection of black beads – tough-looking ones, not girly ones.

Thom's birthday was coming up so I made him a necklace out of the stones, starting with the small black beads. I then threaded a small Iona stone, then slightly larger black beads, another larger Iona stone, saving the three largest Iona stones for the centre piece. I gave Thom his birthday present a few days before his birthday.

He asked, "What are they?"

I replied, "They're Iona stones."

"Iona stone. That's a great name for a band."

Anyone Can Play Guitar, off the album *Pablo Honey*, refers to this time. I will get back to this track a little later. There's much more to it than just Jim Morrison and growing my hair.

Even though I was with Sasha, I did see Jackie from time to time. She messed me about a lot, so I didn't take the relationship too seriously. One night she phoned me at the bar, and asked me to come over to her mother's house.

When I left at around 11.20, it was pitch black out. The winter nights were now setting in but it was still quite mild. Being a bit of a show-off, I took the Targa top off my car and put it in the boot. Jackie's mum lived in Carterton, close to the RAF Brize Norton air base. It was about a thirty-minute drive.

As I left Buckland village via St Georges Road, turning onto Buckland Road, I put my foot down and sped off into the night. Just as the road dips slightly, I was about to drop the car into fourth gear and, from out of the corner of my right eye, I noticed a bright orange light. I slowed and turned my head to look. On the right-hand side of Buckland Road there is a woodland. This strange orange light was slowly moving from left to right, up in the top of the trees. I couldn't believe what I was seeing.

As it passed through the branches, the light sort of split into beams, like rays of light. As I was still in fifth gear and slowing down, the engine began to shudder a little. I turned my head and put the car into third and, just like in a movie, when I looked back the light was gone.

Thom came back the following week and, after a few spliffs and a couple of beers, I began telling him about my encounter. I could see by the look on his face that he didn't believe me. We left it at that.

The next week, Thom rang the bar from uni and told me how he had just read about a group of students in the paper who had reported seeing a strange orange light above the woods in Northern France.

When Thom came back, it's all that we could talk about. After a joint or two, our imaginations ran riot. We sat and fantasised about being abducted and taken off into space.

Thom asked, "Paul do you think you could handle it, being abducted?"

"Yer, of course, I'd be okay. What about you?"

Now both of us agreeing that we would be okay, the conversation turned to what we would do once up there. Sasha sat listening to us chatting our stoned nonsense. We didn't care. I told Thom that I'd first visit my hometown and let everyone know that I was on my way to the stars.

Subterranean Homesick Alien, on the album *OK Computer*, released May 1997 – why, you might ask, did I say before that this track was plagiarised? Not only was this my story that I shared with Thom, but I had also written a brief description of the encounter in one of my poetry books. It wasn't a poem yet but my intention was to write it at a later date. The contents of these notes can be found throughout the song.

I wish they'd swoop down in a country lane
Late at night when I'm driving
Take me on board their beautiful ship
Show me the world as I'd love to see it

As I say, there are other references elsewhere in the song so, yes, I think that the word 'plagiarised' fits well in this instance.

Buckland Road, direction Bampton. It can be a very lonely place late at night. To the left in the treetops – just as the hill dips towards you – is where I saw the strange orange light. I was driving down the hill looking over my right shoulder. *Subterranean Homesick Alien* – such a great song.

The title track off the album *The Bends* also focuses on our time at The Lamb Inn, when Thom came on the scene. It was just Sasha and I in the bar most nights. Buckland village is what a townie might call the middle of nowhere. After nine at night the bar would be quiet, so Sasha and I would sit about getting a bit drunk. She didn't smoke pot, but she loved her Bacardi and Coke.

Thom and I had often joked that in the future, one of us would return to the bar – only to find that the other had not made anything of his life, and would be drip-fed straight from the beer taps.

> *Just lying in the bar with my drip feed on*
> *Talking to my girlfriend*
> *Waiting for something to happen*

I mentioned before that I was a bit of a loner. When you work in catering, you meet a lot of people but you don't really have a lot of friends – mostly because you move around a lot. When Thom and I met, we discussed the fact that although we knew a lot of people, we didn't have any real friends. That's another reason why we connected so well – we were both in need of company and support. Isn't that what friends are for?

I have needed support over the years, and I am sure Thom could have done with a bit of reality in his life. None of them corporate pigs or the sycophantic, money-grabbing, so-called supporters could ever be trusted. I have often wondered who the fuck he has had to truly rely on. I was a fuck-up and I followed the wrong path but I know one thing for sure: I am the only true friend Thom has ever had. I was a real friend. I have come to realise over the years that he was never mine.

Who are my real friends?
Have they all got the bends?
Am I really sinking this low?

Thom referring to coming up too quickly is a two-sided comment: The band came up so quick it was as if they had the bends, as mentioned by Gary Crowley during his show *The Beat* on LWT. The bends could also refer to my intake of drugs and the fact that I came up so fast.

Enough of that!

Thom had spoken with the boys about my request to get involved with the band. The next Monday they turned up at the bar. Edward was the one who seemed to be in control. He sort of took charge of the conversation. To be honest I didn't really know what to say. Right from the start I was out of my depth. I gave them all a drink and we sat chatting for a while, discussing their music and where they wanted to take it. Record companies were at the top of the agenda. EMI and Geffen were the first and only two that really got a mention.

Colin then asks me, "So, Paul, what do you hope to gain from this?"

I hadn't really thought about that.

I just said, "Well, I am only really doing this for Thom. I've always wanted to be in a band. Okay this is not how I imagined it, but really I don't know what I want out of it."

Edward then mentions how U2 had given their friend the

manager's job and had cut him in for a share. Everyone agreed that this was a good idea. We all shook hands and the plans were set. Edward was to take back the demo and have another ten copies made. As I was paying for the tapes, I suggested making twenty. I convinced them that I was not going to stop promoting the band until they got a deal, so having twenty copies would save us getting more done in the future, and that I planned on sending them to every record company that I could find. To help me on my way Edward handed me a reference book containing all the necessary contacts.

The following week, I met Edward at the top of Little Clarendon Street to collect the tapes. He handed the box over and I noticed that three of them were missing. He told me that he wanted to keep them for himself. I was a little pissed off, as I was the one paying for them. I asked him if he would like a drink at Bill's Wine Bar, but I already knew the answer.

As we said our goodbyes, he had to have the last word: "Be careful with those demos Paul, don't lose them."

I have to tell you here, that during my time in Buckland village I made friends with everyone, except for PC Plod. Why on earth was it so hard being friends with Edward? I swear to God, I did nothing to hurt or offend him, and yet the more I became involved with the band, the more he seemed to hate me. I thought that I was the one doing him the favour.

I was friendly with his mother, and his sister had invited me to her twenty-first birthday party, despite his protests. The fact is, he wasn't around to celebrate her birthday. To this day,

I have no idea what his problem was. I haven't lost any sleep over it, but it has left me a little baffled.

When I got into Bill's Wine Bar it was packed. I could see that Bill was well stressed out. He told me that his barmaid hadn't turned up for work, so he had to run both the upstairs and the basement bar by himself.

I sprang into action.

"Don't worry Bill. I'll take care of the basement."

I was behind the bar before he had a chance to say no. Bill had a nervous twitch in his neck – when he spoke to you his head would shake side to side, as if he was saying no all the time – and I have already mentioned that I rarely took no for an answer.

When I stepped behind the bar, a group of students let out a mighty cheer.

"At last," one young lady says with a snotty look on her face. "It's my birthday today and we've been waiting ages for a drink."

"Don't worry," I said. "I'm here now."

Thom's demo got its first airing that night at Bill's place. Several people came down from the upstairs bar and asked me who the band was. I played it several times. I felt great telling them that it was a new band from Oxford who I was busy promoting.

I gave the Birthday Girl a couple of free cocktails, and when the bar shut at 2am, we made our way to her dorm at one of the colleges. She sneaked me past the night watchman.

We spent the night going at each other like rabbits – and guess what? I didn't lose the tapes.

Thom and I got busy making the first of two copyrights. The first was a returned, signed and sealed package from the postmaster in the village. Vivian kept it in her safe, and the other was sent to Copyright House in Northwest London. The guys went back to uni and I began putting our plans into action. I started going into Oxford late at night. Raoul's Wine Bar on Walton Street was one of my favourite hangouts. On this particular night, Sean, the DJ lad I have mentioned before, was upstairs in the corner, banging out his weekly dose of acid jazz.

The barman said, "Paul, look up."

I looked up and the whole ceiling was busy buckling due to the weight from the partygoers jumping up and down to Sean's set.

"You had better move against the wall," he said, "Just in case the ceiling falls in."

We all thought that this was amusing. Then, as I turned round, I nearly shat myself. Right behind me – just standing there, saying nothing – was a six-foot skinhead, bleached jeans, flying jacket, boots, the lot. He freaked me out a bit, it just didn't seem normal to stand so close to someone and not say a word.

After seeing the look of horror on my face the skinhead starts to talk to me.

"Hello mate. Where you from?"

"Liverpool." I said. "Hello mate, I'm Paul."

"No, you're not, you're Scouse."

"No mate, I am a Scouse, but my name is Paul."

He then took a swig from his bottle and said, "Look mate, you're from Liverpool so your name is Scouse, I'm Clint."

He held out his hand for me to shake and, after that, everyone in Raoul's started calling me Scouse. Within weeks, everyone who I met in Oxford referred to me as Scouse.

I stood at the bar with Clint until about one in the morning. He then suggested that we go to the Coven nightclub. When we got there it was full of punks, rockabillies, goths and loads of students running about out of their nuts. I went downstairs to the dancefloor with Clint and we had a jump about with the punks and goths. I had a great night.

We made arrangements to meet the following Wednesday in Raoul's. Clint was there with another friend, who he introduced as Groper.

"Ha, ha," Clint says, "He got that name because, when he's had a few drinks, he can't keep his hands off the ladies."

The three of us got on great.

After a few rounds Clint said, "Were going to Downtown Manhattans. Are you coming with us?"

I told them that I'd been to that club a few months before and that it was crap.

"No way Scouse, it's Student Night tonight. It will be packed. The drinks are all half price."

We made our way to the club and he wasn't wrong: the place was bouncing, wall-to-wall chaos, people all our own age running and skipping. I noticed twin girls swapping wigs. I pointed it out to Groper, who knew them.

He said, "Scouse they do that every week, to take the piss out of all the lads."

"What do you mean?"

"You know, they flirt with one guy, and then they change their wigs so that the fella thinks he bought the other one a drink."

Clint, being straight to the point, adds, "Yer, Scouse, they're fuckin fit – but do yourself a favour: stay the fuck away from them."

The next thing, he pulls out a plastic bag with white powder inside.

"Fancy a bit of speed, Scouse?" he says.

We went to the toilet and I took a couple of lines. This is where it started. The drugs, that is. I had smoked a bit of pot, but I always thought that pot was just the same as booze.

Now I am taking chemicals. It wasn't long, and we were in the middle of the dancefloor sweating like fuck, jumping and screaming like everyone else.

This club thing was getting better. I couldn't wait to finish work, take a taxi into town and get out of my nut with the lads. Clint then mentions a rave that he and Groper are going to in Bournemouth.

"Scouse," Clint says. "Have you ever taken an E?"

"What's that?" I asked.

Groper grabs my arm and says, "Scouse you're going to love it. Come with us to Bournemouth and get on one."

The truth was I didn't know what ecstasy was. I had heard about it on TV and it had been mentioned in the papers, but really, I didn't have a clue.

The following Friday, I arranged for Thom and Bailey to look after the bar so that I could go to Bournemouth with the lads.

I had never been to a rave. I asked Thom if he knew anything about them. He told me that he had been to a couple at uni. He helped me pick out the weirdest clothes I had – faded blue jeans and a red paisley shirt. I tucked the shirt into my jeans and laced up my boots.

Thom thought that this was amusing.

"You can't go to a rave looking like that."

He reaches forward, pulls out the shirt tails from the top of my jeans, kneels down in front of me, unties my boot laces and tucks the bottom of my jeans into my boots. He then stands in front of me, and pulls out a blue-and-white fisherman's hat, the Stone Roses kind. He puts it on my head and says, "This is my father's, but you can have it."

He fixes the hat so that it just covers my eyes and he says, "There you go Paul, now you look like a raver."

Clint and Groper then came screeching into the car park, Clint skidding his BMW sideways while his horn blasted away the village silence.

"See you later, Thom," and I was off.

We got to Bournemouth just as it was getting dark and made our way to the Pyramid Club in the centre of town. As we walked down the street we could hear the bass thumping in the distance.

We got closer and the muted thud of the bass got ever so strong. There was no one at the door of the club, just a girl behind a glass screen taking £10 off everyone to get in. We paid, and she pointed to the lift in the corner.

"Take that up to the second floor," she says.

We walked over to the lift and a lovely young lady appears out of nowhere. She was wearing a crop top, denim shorts and a pair of boxing boots. She had her hair in pigtails with different coloured ribbons tied into them. I looked her up and down. She was fucking fit, her crop top revealing a brightly painted torso, blue and yellow patterns painted on her skin.

As we stepped into the lift, she said, "Where are you lads from?"

The three of us said in unison, "OXFORD!"

I am sure that my tongue was hanging out.

The lift door pinged open and I was hit in the face with a blanket of heat. The young lady let out a little scream and I watched as she disappeared into the mass of arms and legs on the dance floor.

The bass was pounding. I stared at the dancefloor. It just looked chaotic, people running and skipping, groups dancing wildly together.

I turned to Clint and said, "It looks like a bowl of spaghetti."

"It will in a minute, Scouse. Here, have one of these," he says, showing me a little bag of white pills. "These are called Doves, Scouse. Here, get one in yer."

I asked Groper what it was going to do to me. "Just take it, Scouse, don't worry. You'll be all right."

We took the pills at the same time and I could soon feel the effects. My jaw felt heavy and I had a happy, confused look on my face. I could see that the optics behind the bar had changed to a sort of chalky colour.

Groper grabs my arm and asks, "Has it got you, Scouse?"

He looks into my eyes. "Oh, fuck me! Yes it has," he shouts to Clint.

It wasn't long, and I became a part of the bowl of spaghetti on the dancefloor.

That was it for me. Raves became my focus. Any night of the week, I would finish work and go in search of a party. I loved every minute of it and the best thing was, we all loved one another. At last, my 1960s had arrived and there was no way that I was missing a thing.

By September 1991 the cops had had enough of the farmers' – and the public's – complaints about the damage and the nuisance caused by revellers. A farmer near Enstone had a whole field of crops damaged by at least two hundred cars, driving across his land at about five thirty in the morning. I know because I was one of the first through it. Slated cabbages all over the place.

Now the cops had powers to turn up mob-handed and confiscate complete sound systems. The clubs soon took advantage of this and they started putting on some great parties. Any night of the week in Oxford I could find a party – but my favourite place was the Arena, just outside the city centre in Cowley. Monday nights bouncing, Wednesday nights bouncing. It didn't matter what night of the week it was in that venue, we always had a good time – even if hardly anyone turned up.

One night I was sitting in the Arena with Clint. We had bought a couple of Es earlier. Someone had told us that DJ Lisa was playing that night. We had heard a few things about Lisa. People said that she only got to play the clubs of Oxford because her uncle owned the Coven nightclub. Because of what we'd heard we didn't rate her as a DJ. Well, we were in for a shock.

Lisa turned up with her entourage. We were surprised but she obviously had a bit of a following. There had been a couple of DJs playing earlier on but, by now, everyone was buzzing about Lisa. Clint and I dropped our Es at the same time.

MC Zachariah steps forward: "Right about now, the one and only DJ Lisa, in the place."

Clint says, "Come on, Scouse. Let's get amongst it."

We made our way across the dancefloor to the raised

platform on the left. Everyone was buzzing. The effects of the Es that we'd just taken soon got a grip on us, my jaw now beginning to ache because I was grinning like a Cheshire cat. Lisa lets a track run as she's getting ready. A slow, growling bass starts to grab our attention. All the lights are out except for the DJ booth. The bass is thumping a little louder, Lisa brings in another track and slowly the whistles start. People are stamping their feet on the wooden platform, the bass and the stamping in unison. I begin stamping too, left right, left right, everyone together as one.

MC Zachariah steps under the fluorescent light wearing a long dark coat and his dark shades. He takes off his coat and his white robes glow brightly as the light hits him. His dreads hanging down his back, he raises his mic.

"Are you ready? Are you ready?!"

The crowd starts blowing whistles, shouting and screaming. The vibe is unbelievable. The Es are rushing up my spine. Everyone is now champing at the bit, and then Zachariah starts:

"L, for an I, for an S, for an A. DJ Lisa's, on her way."

Lisa syncs another track, drops the bass and the whole room goes absolutely fucking mental – running, skipping, screaming, shouting. For hours we danced like wild animals, everyone together, all of us out of our nuts on ecstasy and speed. Dripping with sweat, everyone hugging and kissing – black kids, white kids, Asian kids, half-naked girls and boys, smiling and running about, Clint with his muscles making an appearance.

We left the club early the next morning. For me, that night at the Arena was one of the best I have ever had.

Returning to the village after nights like that, I couldn't help sharing my stories. The papers were still going mad – "This farmer awoke to find this", "This farmer awoke to find that". Almost all the people who came into the bar were farmers, or if not, they were attached to the farming trade. They were fascinated by my wild stories: Cassington with Dean Sinclair and Pandi P on the mic, Enstone, locked in a disused warehouse, Bicester when a group of lads took over a playing field, right in the middle of a council estate.

The Scollio brothers got wise and they started putting parties on out in the middle of the Cotswold countryside. The locals loved my sordid details, none more so than Charlie Wellesley. He often quizzed me on how much money one of these parties could generate. Charlie had loads of land. I did my best to encourage him, but he was having none of it.

With all this talk of anti-social behaviour, it wasn't long before the Witch-hunter General was back on the scene. Someone had put a party on in Tubney Wood, just down the road from Buckland village. I didn't know at the time, but Martin and the other village bobbies had their noses put out of joint because they couldn't contain the rabble. They just had to sit it out while the drugged-up revellers partied the night away.

Now, Martin thinking that it is his noble duty to find

out who the culprits are, comes into the Lamb Inn to question me. The pub was quite packed.

He sits right in front of me on a bar stool and says, "Come on, Paul. I know you know who these people are."

I hadn't even poured his drink.

"What?" I replied.

"You were away last weekend. Did you and your friends put that party on?"

Yet again, I am faced with his bullshit. I told him that I was at my parents' house in Lancashire when the party was on, which was the truth. He was having none of it. The bar went quiet, everyone now listening to him chew my ear off. I had no choice but to defend myself.

"Listen here, Martin. I had fuck all to do with that party and, even if I did, I wouldn't tell you a fuckin thing."

There were a few sniggers and jeers from behind him. He just smiled at me, then he struck up a conversation with some other poor sod.

Thom phoned and I told him about my nights out – in particular, Downtown Manhattans. I suggested that we go there for a night out.

"What about the others?" he asked.

"The band?" I replied,

"Yes, Colin, Phil and Jonny," he said. No mention of Edward.

When Thom got back from uni, we arranged to meet the others at Raoul's Wine Bar on Walton Street. Thom being a little embarrassed tells me that they didn't really have enough money to go clubbing. I told him not to worry, that I would sort the money out.

When I arrived at Raoul's, the boys were already sitting upstairs. We hit the bar quite hard for the first hour, relaxing and having fun. Thom and I began mimicking playing the trumpet along with one of the tracks that Sean had on downstairs. Thom then mimics a saxophone solo while I am making trumpet sounds with my mouth. We are now rocking side to side. Phil gives Thom a look, just a little glance, and Thom shuts up immediately. I didn't really think about it at the time.

A few days later I asked Thom why he had stopped. He just said, "Well they're not into that sort of thing."

"What, they're not into having a laugh?"

He told me that's just the way they were.

At about 10pm we made our way to Downtown Manhattans. Dean Sinclair's dad ran the door. I was chuffed when he let us in straight away. No need to queue up with the others. As we are walking down the stairs Thom asks me how I know him.

"Just from coming here, that's all."

I told him that Clint, Groper and I were now getting a bit of a reputation as mad heads, me especially.

As we made our way down the stairs I was a bit concerned the club was going to be quiet after all the hype that I'd given it – but I wasn't disappointed. As usual, it was rocking, indie tunes with a good mix of punk, grunge and goth tracks thrown in. I gave Thom thirty quid and he and the others shot off across the dance floor. I didn't care about that. I had already told them that my mate Clint was on his way down. I ordered a drink and over my left shoulder, I heard a familiar voice.

"Now then, Scouse."

Clint had arrived with one of his other friends, Harvey. We said our hellos and Clint mentioned that Harvey's friends were also in a band called the Blue Fields.

Now me being Oxford's newest music promoter (whatever), I say to Harvey, "Tell your friends that I will call in and see them."

I really was beginning to believe my own bullshit.

Thom comes running over.

"Paul, Paul can I have another twenty quid? We're with some girls, I want to buy them a drink?"

I was made up for him so I gave him the twenty quid and away he ran. Just months before, we had had a discussion on how to talk to girls. He really didn't have a clue. He was really worried that they would think he was only trying to get into their knickers.

I said to him, "That's exactly what you are trying to do. It's just how you go about it that makes all the difference."

I told him to talk to girls just as he would talk to boys. Ask them what they're doing at uni. What they're studying for, that sort of thing.

I went on. "Just show that you're interested in what

they're doing. Most girls love the attention, and not every girl you meet will automatically think that you're trying to get into her knickers."

A couple of weeks after this conversation Thom phoned me from uni, all excited, telling me how he'd done what I had said. He had walked up to one of the girls who he liked in his class and he started chatting with her.

"Paul, we got on so well. We even had our lunch together."

Now here he is in the club chatting up the birds. I was made up for him, and the girl who he had lunch with, he married her.

Clint and Harvey left, and I waited at the top of the stairs for the lads. We took a taxi back to their student house. I was really surprised when I walked inside. These lads coming from really well-to-do families, actually lived like *The Young Ones*. It was the first student house that I had ever been into, so I was ignorant to the fact that it was more like a party house and a place to crash than home.

Trying to make light of the situation, I turned to Colin and said, "Fuck me Colin, if I was you I would sack your cleaner."

"We don't have a cleaner, Paul," came the reply. My attempt at humour was wasted on him.

Incidentally, Colin recently released a book called *How to Disappear - A Portrait of Radiohead*. I went on my X / Twitter account and searched for Colin to read about his book release – as I had done with Edward when he brought out his solo album, *Earth*, in 2020. To my surprise, it seems Colin has searched for me on X and blocked me from tweeting him or viewing his profile. Despite me not having my name visible, he found my account @pablohoney20. It's obvious someone has been talking about me. Honestly, I have never made any attempt to contact him or message him since 1991.

That night I slept in the back room on the ground floor. The next morning I awoke to the sound of Edward's voice. I quickly got up and sorted myself out. Edward came into my room, guitar in hand. I sat next to him on the small couch and he played a track by Neil Young. I was well impressed. He had a bit of a voice on him as well.

Then, just like that he says, "Paul don't you think it would be best if you got something down on paper? You know, to protect your position."

I reminded him that I was really only doing this for Thom. He went on to tell me how much of a backstabbing business the music industry was. I was really surprised at what he was saying. Maybe I was wrong about him – that did go through my mind at the time. If I had any clue about the music business, I would have had them sign a contract or something but, seriously, that sort of thing never entered my head. I was having a laugh with my mate – and doing him a favour at the same time. That's all it was to me.

Thom and I left their student house about thirty minutes later. Thom was driving his father's Morris Minor at the time.

We made our way back to Buckland. The car was getting on a bit and the fact that half of it was made of wood didn't do the engine much good. It would only do about 45 miles per hour and that was with the wind behind it. We drove past Tubney Wood and on the left-hand side of the road, in the lay-by, was the regular flower seller. This guy would park there in the morning and would work until late, selling small bouquets and roses.

"Here Thom, listen," I said, sighting a sign at the side of the road. "*Fresh-cut flowers, arranged and sold, £1.50 to show I care, £1.50 to my lover lure.*"

"What, just like that?" he says.

"Ha, Ha," I just laughed.

"You won't be laughing when you see what's behind us."

I looked back and there was a trail of cars going back as far as the eye could see. We were too busy laughing and joking – we had no idea what was going on behind us.

This section of the A420 was still single-file traffic and it was virtually impossible for anyone to overtake safely. The panic set in for both of us. Thom gripped the steering wheel tight and let out a scream of defiance.

"I'm going as fast as I fuckin can!"

He was leaning forward slightly, gripping the wheel even tighter.

"Come on, come on." He urged the car to go faster, but it was no use. A couple of cars took the chance and overtook us, blasting their horns and hurling abuse as they went past.

Thom says, "I'm going to make a bumper sticker of a hedgehog saying, "Fuck off – I'm going as fast as I can."

This was long before anyone had ever produced such a bumper sticker. Over the years, I would laugh with Sasha, saying, "Look, Thom designed that. He is an artist after all."

That afternoon, just as I was cleaning up the bar, Thom's father comes in. By now he had heard of my involvement with the band and he obviously felt a little worried at the way things were going. The conversation went something like this:

"Hello, Mr Yorke. Would you like a drink?"

"No Paul, I am not here for a drink. I am here to ask you to stop filling Thom's head with this music nonsense. Under no circumstances is he dropping out of uni to pursue a career in music."

"Mr Yorke, Thom has no intention of dropping out of uni."

"Okay Paul, make sure that it stays that way."

He turned to leave, as he was about to exit the bar, I called behind him.

"Mr Yorke, I really do think that Thom and the band will make it."

"Not every band makes it Paul. Just see to it he finishes his degree."

Thom's dad left. I had been warned.

I was using more and more drugs while the lads were back at uni. Ecstasy was my main drug of choice. The lads were due back for a week's break so I arranged with Thom to meet them all at the Blue Boar pub in Longworth Village that coming Monday.

I had sent the demo to a few record companies and I had badgered several A&R guys. One guy, Ian, said that he would listen to the demo. but he was taking weeks to get back to me. I bugged the life out of him. The poor sod had had enough of me leaving messages on his answer machine.

He called me and said, "I will listen to it over the weekend, I promise. Please don't call again until next week."

Another girl, Polly at Geffen Records, told me that she was impressed with the demo and she asked for the band's gig list. I was overjoyed. I couldn't wait to tell the boys and now, having four gigs booked, I was sure that I could just sit back and wait for the whole thing to take off.

I made my way into Oxford that Saturday night and met Clint early in the evening at Bill's Wine Bar on Little Clarendon Street. We made our way to the Arena, and when we got there, Clint knew the doorman. He told us not to bother that night, apparently everyone had gone to Roots in the town centre.

Roots was an old, abandoned church that had been done up by a group of Rastafarians. They fought long and hard to get the club up and running. Now it was party night.

We jumped in a taxi and made our way back into town.

Clint had already bought us two Es each. Now, as this was going to be a long night, when we got into Roots we went around the dealers and bought a further four Es each. We went to the bar and ordered a drink. Clint says, "How many you got, Scouse?"

"Six," I replied.

"Which ones shall we do first?"

"All of them." And with that, I swallowed the lot down with a bottle of Becks.

Clint said, "Fuck it," and followed suit.

I don't remember too much about that night but what I can recall is standing in the middle of the dance floor with my left arm stretched out above the top of my head. In my mind I was holding on tight to a section of my skull that had morphed into the shape of a jigsaw puzzle. A tremendous gust of wind was blowing back and forth from the puzzle piece inside my hand to the hole in the side of my head. This jigsaw piece, I knew, fitted perfectly into my head and I tried and tried to put it back in. In my mind, I knew that if I let go, I was finished.

Other than when I came round a few hours later I only remember seeing Clint the once. He ran up to me and he screamed into my face.

"I'm out my fuckin mind!"

Sally and Ellie, the two girls who worked at Mahogany Hair Salon in Oxford came to our rescue. Sally took Clint and she sat him down in the bar. Ellie then came over to me and took me by the hand. Not the one holding the piece of jigsaw. As she walked me back to the bar, everyone was looking at me. I had the horrors at this point.

Ellie calmly says, "Scouse, take your hand off your head, everyone's looking at you."

And just like that, it was as if my eyes had re-opened. I was in a terrible state. To this day, Clint still swears that he had an outer-body experience. I have no idea what I went through but with behaviour like that it's no wonder my relationship with Thom was doomed. I went from being his best and only friend to nothing more than his gimmick.

I spent the day after with Clint. Both of us were doing our best to recover from the traumatic events of the night before. We drank for most of that Sunday and we smoked spliff after spliff – I suppose in some way to smother the downer that was now creeping in.

I made my way back to Buckland that evening and tried to sleep but it was no use. I phoned Clint, he was back out on the piss so I called a taxi and went to meet him. We didn't take any Es but we sniffed enough speed to kill a horse.

Monday was now here. I had to try and get my head together to meet the lads at The Blue Boar. There was no way that I was going to be able to sleep and, in the morning, I could feel cold sores growing on my lower and upper lips. When you're out of your nut and something like a cold sore starts to bug you, you end up chewing your face off. So when I arrived at the meeting

I was a fucking mess to say the least: blood-shot eyes, white as a sheet and I had been wearing the same clothes since Saturday night. I had had no sleep at all, my mouth was full of blisters. I was still out of my mind. We sat together and, right from the start, I could see that I was making them feel uncomfortable.

I did my best to appear coherent, but it was no use. I couldn't control myself. Within minutes I was jumping down Colin's throat as soon as he opened his mouth.

"No! No! Listen to me, we're not doing that, we're doing this. No, no here listen …"

The thing was, I really had nothing to say. I could have cancelled the meeting and I could have told them what was going on the next day, but I was unable at this point to make any normal decisions. What I did have to say, I couldn't properly convey.

I told them about the gigs: the Holly Bush, the Fire Station, the Co-op Hall, Jericho Tavern – all completely in the wrong order. I then went on and on about this girl called 'Penny' at Geffen Records. Edward would later remind me that there was no such girl at Geffen called Penny.

I could see I was annoying them, but no matter what I did I was fucked, and they knew it. I really couldn't convey anything of real value and, like I said, there was no need for any of us to be there. I was obnoxious, ridiculous, and all the other dreadful words that end in -ous, combined. Even now, when I think back to that night and the way that I made everyone feel – including myself – it makes my skin crawl.

Seriously. I am cringing while writing this. No wonder they got shut of me.

How Do You?, track 3 on *Pablo Honey*, focuses on this time:

> *He wants you to listen*
> *He wants us to weep*
> *And he was a stupid baby*
> *Who turned into a powerful freak*

The Blue Boar pub: where I put the living shits into the band due to my out-of-control, drug-fuelled behaviour. Even in 2018, when I was driving into Longworth village to take this picture my gut was turning. The thoughts that I have about this place still give me the creeps.

The Holly Bush in Oxford: the second gig that I booked for
'On a Friday'

My relationship with Thom still seemed to be ok, despite my outbursts. Before, when I said that I became nothing more than Thom's gimmick, I meant it and I am sure by then he was just keeping me around to draw attention to the band. No matter how ridiculous my behaviour, he knew that I would get the job done.

Around this time, Thom came into the bar with his younger brother Andy. Andy was a real cool customer, tall, long hair, good looking, confident, a total opposite from Thom. He was also crazy about music. We shared our passion for The Doors. We spent the whole day and night getting to know one another, the three of us well and truly pissed and stoned by 3am. After that it was time for me to get some sleep. I had the local shoot the next morning, and I always liked looking after them as they were all Michael's friends.

Thom and Andy got themselves together to leave. I packed the rest of my pot in one last spliff, handing it to Thom for their epic journey back home about eight minutes away. They left and I finally crashed out.

The next afternoon Thom arrived.

"Where's Andy?" I asked.

"I've come to see you alone Paul."

I could see that there was something on his mind. I asked him what was wrong.

We sat beside the bar and Thom began to tell me what had happened after they'd left in the early hours.

"Paul, Andy and I didn't make it home last night. We only got as far as the Croft. We climbed the fence and lay in the field smoking that spliff that you made for us. We didn't get home until after six. We lay there stoned watching the sun come up."

I listened intently because I knew that something was coming. I had known him long enough by now to know that something was bugging him. He went on.

"Andy and I were talking about him replacing Edward in the band."

I wasn't really surprised; Thom had mentioned before how Edward was not much of a guitarist. He went on.

"Edward is far too tall. He just doesn't fit in with the rest of us."

I thought about this for a minute, and then I reminded him about the visit from his father.

"Look Thom, I don't think that it's a good idea. Andy has a further two years of uni left. Can you imagine how your dad's going to react to both of you being in the band?"

Thom thought about it for a while. He then decided to leave it at that. We didn't talk about it again. Edward didn't need to know. Can you imagine, Edward might have reached the dizzying heights of Manager at Browns Café if I had carried out Thom's wishes. There's no way that he would have made any money playing his guitar.

He now wears sandals or goes barefoot when he's on stage. I often wondered if that was Thom's doing.

This is the Croft where Thom and his brother Andy spent the early hours getting stoned and making plans for Edward's exit from the band. God knows how many years that gate has been there – nothing much has changed in the village.

The title *2 + 2 = 5*, track 1 off the album *Hail To The Thief*, came about when I started deluding myself that I would be better suited to the band than Edward, knowing that Thom was not too keen on keeping him around. I began convincing myself that I could replace him. One night after a session with Thom in the bar I went up to my apartment. I was watching the *Open University* programme late in the evening. This episode was dedicated to mathematics. The bearded boffins were discussing the possibility that a sum could truly be impossible within light, space, time and so on.

I wrote my poetry about things that happened on a daily basis. Things that also consumed my imagination. The idea that Thom wanted Edward out of the band planted a seed firmly in my head – not right away – but I think that, secretly, I wanted to be in the band for real, not just on the sidelines.

Watching that programme, I began to write my thoughts at the top of the page. I wrote what I thought to be my impossible sum: 2 + 2 = 5. Edward leaving the Band would leave 2 + 2; me replacing him would once again make five, as simple as that. It wasn't even the name of the poem – I hadn't given it a name because I never got round to finishing it. I wrote '2 + 2 = 5' at the top of the page as a reminder, just as I'd done many times before with lots of my poems.

Are you such a dreamer
To put the world to rights
I'll stay home forever
where 2 + 2 always makes up 5

I was a dreamer and so was Thom. Our dreams were set in motion right there in that bar. I had helped make Thom's wishes come true. He struggled with everything. I may see myself as his one-time genie, his wish-giver. I am sure that, if or when he gets to read this, he will see me as nothing more than a nasty little leprechaun, back from the bushes in search of a pot of gold.

Really though, I've always made my own money. This book is written for my own gains, of course. Thom has never given me anything, not even a thank-you. Chris Hufford would never have picked them up at the Jericho Tavern if it wasn't for me. Where's the thanks for that? None of the money that I gave him was ever paid back, despite his promises. Not a word of credit for any of my poetry, songs or lyrics. All he has done is taken what he can without so much as a "Kiss my arse".

He has focused on my life so much that it's disturbing. He didn't have a life, so I suppose he thought, "Fuck it, Paul is not interested in his life, so I will focus on it and claim it for my own."

Lots of people over the years have said this to me: "Yer, but Paul, that could just be a coincidence."

I'll tell you about coincidence. The album, *In Rainbows* – is this a coincidence? Where I lived in Skelmersdale in Lancashire, when I was about six or seven, I used to go out the front of the house and keep the driveway clean for my mum. I would run the hosepipe from the downstairs toilet and out through the front door. Our house had three floors and I worked out that if I stood just beside the shadow being cast by the house, and pressed my finger over the end of the hose to create a fine spray, the sun shining over the rooftop would create a rainbow when hitting the spray. I could sometimes completely surround myself with a rainbow if I spun round quickly enough. I would go back into the house soaking wet and my mother would shout at me, "What the bloody hell have you been up to?!"

I replied in my young Scouse accent, "I've been dancing in rainbows."

I mentioned earlier about Thom's use of KID A, well stories of my dancing in rainbows – and many more – were shared with Thom throughout our time together.

Just recently I found out that Radiohead has a song called *Jigsaw Falling into Place*. I had to laugh at that but not in a good way. Coincidence, my arse.

Mum and Dad's house in Skelmersdale. On the driveway is where I danced in rainbows.

I spoke with Thom about getting some studio time booked. He told me that Edward knew a guy named David Smith who lived not far from Buckland and had a studio in his house. I promised Thom that I would visit him to try and arrange a booking. I remember not having a clue what I was talking about. Thom told me about some old Leslie speakers that would spin when the sound going through them was loud enough. When I met David, I start talking about these "Suzi" Speakers (SUZI!). It was some time later that I realised my mistake. No wonder he just looked at me with a grin on his face when I talked to him. He must have thought, "Who *is* this fuckin clown?"

Things were now becoming worse between me and Edward. One time, I arranged to meet the band at Bill's Wine Bar on Little Clarendon Street. I arrived coming down off a couple of nights of taking speed and Es. I made my way to the basement bar. The lads were not sitting together, there were about twenty people there. I sat with Thom and Edward's girlfriend. I was feeling a little paranoid because I was coming down, and also because I'd been a bit of a dickhead the last couple of times we'd met. It's funny now, but this meeting was about to go to shit, too. Even so, Thom wrote the track *Creep* off the album *Pablo Honey* partly about this meeting at Bill's Wine Bar.

Edward's girlfriend was originally from Glasgow. Every now and then she would jump from her English accent back to her Glaswegian accent. I asked her to say "Great" a couple of times. The way that it sounds in a Glaswegian accent is funny, so Thom and I sat having a laugh with her. Little did I know that Edward was watching us and he was getting more and more pissed off. He calls her over to him. The next minute she shouts at him and then she runs up the stairs with Edward slowly following her. As he got to the stairs everyone was staring at him because he had made a scene.

I then commented, "That's love, that."

Edward was now incensed.

"Don't you talk to me, Paul. You don't know me and you don't know my girlfriend."

He then storms up the stairs after her. Now everyone is looking at me. I'm already a bit paranoid and now this. I slump back in my chair, the look of unease on my face.

Thom asks, "You okay Paul?"

"No Thom."

"Why, what's up?"

Would you believe me if I said my answer went something like this: "I dunno. I just feel as if I don't belong here."

"What do you mean?" he asks.

"I just feel like a creep. A fuckin weirdo."

"Because of Edward?"

"It's not just that Thom, but what the fuck is his problem?"

"He's just pissed off that the gigs are so soon. He thinks that we should wait a bit longer before we start gigging. He keeps saying that we're not ready."

I then asked Thom if I should cancel the first gig at the Fire Station.

"No, don't cancel anything."

"But what about Edward?"

"Take no notice of him Paul."

So I didn't.

A couple of lads put a party on in a place called Headington in Oxford. It was a large house in the middle of a really nice estate. I went with my mate, Manny. He was a six-foot, taekwondo, kick-arse motherfucker, as cool as could be. When we got there, I pulled out a bag containing ten wraps of speed.

He asks me, "How much did you pay for that, Scouse?"

"One hundred pounds. Ten pound each," I replied.

"You're fuckin mad, Scouse. You can get a big bag off the travellers for eighty quid."

The next day Manny took me to the travellers' site beside Oxford railway station. Two travellers called us onto their bus. Manny introduced me and I bought twenty-eight grams for eighty quid. An ounce. I couldn't believe it. When I got back to The Lamb, I made it into thirty £10 wraps – eighty quid into three hundred quid, just like that.

The next Wednesday, I made my way into town and, apart from the couple that I had snorted, I sold them all in about an hour.

This is when I started to think about leaving The Lamb and selling drugs for a living. *With a mark-up like that*, I thought, *Why the fuck am I working all week?*

I wanted to party all the time. The Lamb was getting in the way of that. If there was a full weekender, I could only stay for a night, and then I would have to get back for work. I hitchhiked down the A34 one morning and still made it back in time. I loved The Lamb but it was now becoming a bit of a strain, partying all week and staying focused enough to run the place. I was falling apart but I didn't care. The expression 'burning the candle at both ends' comes to mind. The only difference is, I burnt my candle in the middle as well. The self-saboteur inside me was rearing his ugly head, and it wouldn't be long before I would once again be on the move.

One night I was at the Coven nightclub. I was on my own, standing at the side of the dancefloor when this young lad comes running over.

"Hey are you Scouse, Manny's mate?"

"Yes, why?"

"Some Arsenal fans are beating his mate up at the door."

The next thing I know this guy Martin comes running past with five boys chasing him. I didn't know Martin – but I knew that he was a mate of Manny's. I ran over. Martin was much smaller than I was, and here he is trying to fight off these five fuckin shitbags. I flew in and punched a couple of them still – that's when you crack someone just hard enough to straighten them out. My dad taught me that one.

We ended up back-to-back at the door of the club. Martin had two of his student friends with him who lived in a shared house in Tottenham. They weren't football fans – they were students for fuck's sake – but that's why these Arsenal fans wanted to kick their heads in: because they lived in Tottenham. Fuckin shithouses.

The two lads with Martin ran out and brought their car to the front of the club. About four other fights had broken out at this point. Me and Martin were in the thick of it. One of the Arsenal lads was out of his nut trying to punch everyone. He then grabs Martin. Before he has a chance to hit him, I pull him away and smash him as hard as I can. His face bursts open and blood runs from his eye down his left cheek. I caught him with a cracker. The signet rings that I'm wearing are what splits him open. That's it. The bouncers now run in and they start trying to break us up. Martin grabs me from behind and pulls me into the car. We speed off into the night.

Martin and I quickly became friends. I soon learnt that most of the hash in Oxford came from this little fucker.

One afternoon I was walking down Walton Street to meet him and he says, "I can't go into town yet." He pulls up his shirt, "I have to drop this at Manny's house."

Martin had a kilo of hash down the front of his trousers – just blatantly walking down the street. He didn't give a shit.

By today's standards a kilo of hash is nothing; you can buy one from around seven hundred quid. Back then, a kilo was worth up to £2,500 depending on where you lived and, without a doubt, if the coppers caught you with it, you were on your way to jail.

Martin and I went out that evening and all that we spoke about was selling drugs and where we could buy them. I started dealing even before I left The Lamb. The money was ridiculous.

Once the drug dealing started, it wasn't long before a network started to form. It's not something that you plan, it's just that you attract like-minded people. Within a couple of weeks, through Martin I had met most of the up-and-coming gangsters. Martin was quick to let them know that I was a bit of a handful and the story of my super-hero tactics rescuing him from the Arsenal fans went around like wildfire. I was getting a bit of a reputation and, to be honest, I loved it.

I started carrying a 10-inch, Rambo-style knife down the back of my trousers – I got that idea from the movie *The Krays* starring the Kemp brothers – and I made sure that everyone knew I had it.

One of the local doormen, nicknamed Gruff, was a lump and a half. Well, he owed me 275 quid and he was taking weeks to pay me. By now I was buying all the drugs, and Martin and a few others were running about selling the stuff. Gruff thinking that he is a bit of a tough guy tells Martin over the phone, "Tell Scouse he'll just have to wait for his fuckin money."

I was on a serious comedown when Martin came back from the phone and told me what he said – and when I am tired I am at my worst. I was sat with the Scollio brothers – four brothers originally from Italy, cool as fuck and well respected on the rave scene. Tony, the eldest, says to me:

"I know where that prick lives. He's still at his mother's house, around the corner from my dad's."

That was it. We ordered a taxi. Then Tony's brothers wanted to get in on the action, so we had to order a second taxi. Outside Gruff's mother's house was a large fern tree – it was massive. I pushed myself back into it so that Gruff wouldn't see me. Tony knocked at the door and Gruff comes out, walking past me to the front gate. I appear behind him, my hand in my right pocket. I didn't have the Rambo knife on me, I had a 9-inch flick knife. I didn't pull it out, I just kept my hand ready to give it to him if needs be. I didn't have to; the confrontation was too much for him.

"Look Scouse, I don't have any money at this minute but come back tomorrow. I have a gun you can have. I don't have any bullets for it. You can take that for the money I owe you."

I suppose that I am still a bit sick in the head because I am finding this whole affair funny even now. This guy was fuckin massive and no doubt he could have kicked the living shits out of me.

He later went around telling people that I had turned up mob-handed at his mother's house and pulled a shooter on him. I didn't care, my reputation was going through the roof.

PC Martin Holder finally got his own back the night I went to Reading Casino in one of Michael's motors. When PC Daft Arse found out where I had gone, and in whose car, he summoned one of his traffic-officer friends (who just happened to be one of the coppers who had lost out to the rabble at Tubney Wood). They drove round the village for hours, around and around they went from about 9.30pm until around 12.30am. I arrived back at the junction to Buckland, and there they were. They came straight after me, following me into the pub car park and breathalysing me. I failed, so they took me to Faringdon Police Station.

Oh, he was ever so fucking pleased with himself.

The young officer couldn't get the Lion intoximeter to work so it was about 2am when I blew 38, just over the legal limit. I had no idea what the legal limit was, and I certainly had no idea about the law.

I was sitting near the front desk, Martin, his traffic-cop friend, the custody sergeant and a young officer stood in front of me. The custody sergeant says, "Listen Mac," like he was my mate. "We are all tired and it's getting late, so there's no need to call a doctor, is there? You're obviously over the limit."

That was his sly pig-arsed way of telling me that I had the right to ask a doctor to take a blood test, and by the time the doctor got there, I believe that I would have been well under the legal limit.

I just said to him, "I don't need a doctor, I'm fine."

Martin, I remember, clapped his hands together rubbing them from side to side.

"Right," he said. "We can all go home now."

As I said before, this is why, as children, we grew up hating coppers. Back in the 70s and 80s, this is the very same behaviour that the police got up to. You didn't know the law – they did, and they fucked you over at every turn. Now here we were in the 90s, and these village bobbies still worked with that same contempt for anyone they chose. That's why we call them fuckin pigs. They have a duty to uphold the law, not to manipulate you – or it – just to satisfy their glorious fucking ego.

Michael came to see me the next morning. Martin, again following police protocol, phones him at 7am to tell him that he'd had me in custody the night before. Can you imagine any copper getting away with that today?

Michael was not happy at all. I had had too many run-ins with Martin, and now the drunk driving. He told me that if the police came to the bar or to his house one more time, I would have to leave.

A couple of days passed, and I got the band over for what was supposed to be their first official photo shoot. I had arranged it with Colin's friend who lived in Abingdon. Thom and I discussed a few days before how Echo and the Bunnymen went into Sefton Park in Liverpool at night and took some pictures, one of them being chosen for their album *Crocodiles* with Ian McCullough crawling on his elbows looking through the undergrowth.

I suggested to Thom that we take some photos behind the old barn. When Colin's friend turned up we made our way across the car park. This is when I handed the lyrics of *High and Dry* to Edward.

"Here, Edward, I've written a song."

I had decided to give them to him as I didn't want Thom thinking that I was trying to outdo him.

He read the lyrics and replied, "It rhymes Paul, I'll give you that."

He took that piece of paper with him and, four years later, *High and Dry* was released as a single off the album *The Bends*.

It has been reported that it's the only song Thom was not happy about having on the album. Not happy? How the fuck do you think I felt?

The photographer went into the barn and set up a black velvet sheet, hanging it from the wall. I was already around the back of the barn with Thom. We went to the front and Colin was ready for his photos. I asked the guy if he would take them in the wooded area at the back of the building. The look on his face, you would think that he'd just caught me fingering his sister. I was having none of it. Jonny, I could see, was really uncomfortable. The guy says to me, "Yes, but the light is perfect in here."

To which I snapped, "If I wanted you to take pictures indoors, why the fuck would I have asked you to come all the way out here?"

That was the second-to-last nail going into my coffin. I had upset everyone again, only this time I thought that they were a gang of whinging pussies. I told Thom how I felt about them that evening.

Thom said, "They're not pussies, Paul. I just think that they're a little afraid of you."

I had not only had enough of The Lamb at this point – I had had enough of these crying arses. Not Thom. As I said before, I didn't even know the others but every time we met, it ended with me looking like a monster.

At the back of this barn – now a flat – is where I wanted to take the first promo pictures of the band. Me and my big mouth fucked that day up as well. There are a few pictures floating about on the internet of Thom and the boys hanging around in the woods, but I never got to see all the photos that were taken that day. I did get to hear the lyrics to *High and Dry* though. Lucky me.

The Cold Rooms at the top end of Cumnor village were a disused meat-packing factory. The fridges were rented out as rehearsal rooms. Thom had booked them so that the band could get ready for their first gig at the Fire Station. Thom gave me directions and I told him that I would come over when they were just about finished.

As soon as I walked in, Edward stopped playing. And then the band stopped. I had brought them drinks and snacks. I put them on the table and when I turned around Edward was walking out the door, guitar in hand.

"Edward!" I called after him. "Where are you going?"

"Oh, I have an appointment. I have to leave."

I immediately thought, *No it's because you're embarrassed about your guitar playing*.

Thom later told me that Edward had already said that if I turned up at the rehearsal room, he was going to leave. I didn't give a shit about his inability to play the guitar – that was Thom's business, I just wanted to know that they were ready, that's all.

I picked up Thom's Fender Telecaster. I would never do that these days – I know how protective people can be over their guitars. I began to strum a few chords. I suppose that I was trying to show Thom that I could actually play the guitar, with the notion still growing in my head that I could replace Edward. It seemed like the right thing to do. Colin, Phil, Jonny and Thom just glared at me, that look of, "How Dare You?". It was not the right thing to do. I put the guitar back on its stand.

I turned to Thom and said, wait for it: "Anyone can play guitar."

Thom wrote *Anyone Can Play Guitar* and put it on the album *Pablo Honey*, track six. Everything that song is here in this story – I'm not going to include any of the lyrics here. I would like you to have a listen to the song and make up your own minds.

I am done trying to convince people. I am either believed or I am not. It doesn't really make much difference to me. If you are a Radiohead fan, you will already be calling me all kinds. If you're not a Radiohead fan you may anyway think that I am completely delusional. All that I can say to you at this stage is, things are going to get much worse. If you can handle it, stick with it, but if you are the timid sort – the quiet, reserved Radiohead fan – it might be best for you to put this book down now because when I say it's going to get much worse, I am not joking. Serious, sinister, dangerous and extremely fucking creepy, are the words that I would choose.

My relationship with the band was now already doomed. My idiotic behaviour saw to that. Their first gig was upon us. I had the record companies buzzing. Everyone I met in Oxford would ask me about On a Friday. The Candyskins and The Jennifers were about the biggest bands in Oxford at the time. The Jennifers were in transition, re-emerging as Supergrass. Meanwhile, The Blue Fields were getting a name for themselves – how they never made it big, I'll never know – but Thom's band was all people could talk about. I knew they were going to make it from the start and now the way that everyone was talking about them I thought, *Right, tickets, I need tickets.* I called the Fire Station and asked the manager to print me 200 tickets. I thought that I could sell a few before the gig. I shared them out with the band, but I ended up on a three-day bender with my Spanish mate and his brother-in-law.

The night of the gig, I arrived at the Fire Station, my two Spanish mates in tow. The lads were still setting up their equipment, so I stayed out of the way. I had pissed them off the last few times that we'd met so I didn't want to create any sort of outburst from Moody Knickers (Edward).

I sat in the corner having a couple of drinks. We did sell a few tickets, sixteen to be precise. Sixteen at two quid a pop. The lads started their set. I looked over and I was made up to see The Candy Skins standing at the bar. We said hello, and then Thom says over the mic: "Have you noticed how so many people in Oxford are full of shit?"

The band then burst into the track *Stop Whispering*. They only performed four songs that night, playing *You* at the beginning and at the end of the set. Their photographer friend was there, buzzing about the stage taking pictures.

When the lads finished their short set, I walked over to speak to Thom. The rest of the band went into a side room. I knew what was coming.

Thom puts his guitar in its case. He steps to the front of the stage and says, "Paul, I didn't think that you were here."

"Of course I was here, Thom. I just stayed out the way so that you could get on with it. Great gig by the way – you sound amazing."

"Thanks Paul. Listen mate, we have been talking and we think that it's best if we go it alone from here."

"Sound Thom," I replied. "I was thinking the same thing."

That really was the truth. I couldn't control my drug use and I knew that it wouldn't be long before I left Buckland. Everything seemed a bit overwhelming. I was exhausted all the time, living on speed and booze, smoking pot like another person would smoke cigarettes. I was a mental wreck at this point.

What was to come over the next few years, it's a wonder that I am still alive.

I told him not to forget the money for the ticket sales, even though it was only thirty-two quid. I knew that he needed it. He asked me to talk to the manager. I went into the office and collected the money. I put in an extra thirty quid, and I went back to the stage and gave it to Thom. I asked him if he wanted to come out with me for a few drinks but he declined. He said that he would see me in the bar the following day.

He never came to the bar again. The next time I saw him was on Abingdon Road in the summer of 1994. This meeting would give him the fuel for the track *The Tourist* off the album *OK Computer*.

As I was leaving the Fire Station, I saw that Edward had parked the van he had hired outside the front door. He was walking in as I walked out. I politely asked him if he wanted to come for a drink but, again, I already knew what his response would be.

"No thanks, Paul. I have to go somewhere."

I made my way to Downtown Manhattans and drank myself into a stupor.

The Old Fire Station. This is the place where we parted company in November 1991. I was so sure that we would see one another again but I was mistaken. That was the difference between Thom and me: I was a true friend to him.

I settled down a little after that and I tried to get my head together. I still went out, but only once or twice a week – and the all-nighters had stopped completely. I was still taking Es, I couldn't stop, not right away anyway. I loved them too much. There was also something – or should I say someone – who I was in love with, Sasha.

I asked her what she would do if I left the village. "I would come with you," she replied.

That was it. My mind was made up. It was time to leave.

I put the word about in Oxford that I was looking for somewhere to live. Clint called me and said that the back room in his house on Juxon Street would be free in a few weeks. I could have that if I wanted.

I was still on good terms with Michael and his family, so I began plotting my escape from the village. I thought, *If I tell Michael that the cops have been again, he would ask me to leave.* So that's what I decided to do.

I had an argument with Sasha in the kitchen one night and in a drug-fuelled rage I smashed my fist through her Bacardi and Coke. The glass almost severed two of my fingers, blood spurting all over the kitchen. She screamed her head off. I went to the bar and one of the regulars, Jimmy Jewel, sorted me out. He had had some trauma training when he was in the Air Force so he bandaged me up pretty good. I went to the hospital and came back wearing a sling, plastered to my elbow.

Michael told me to take some time off. He got a temp in to cover the kitchen and he and his wife Pam ran the bar. A few days later, Michael invited me and Sasha to the horse trials at Lockhinge. Having a picnic out the back of his Mercedes sounded like fun.

We got to Lockhinge and Michael positioned the car at the top of the hill so that we could watch the races. Pam and Sasha got the picnic ready. Michael and I picked out the horses who we were betting on and I walked down the hill and placed the bets. When I came back up I sat next to Sasha. Michael gave me a glass of champagne.

Sasha then taps me on the arm and says, "Look who's coming."

I had already seen them. Edward and Phil came sloping up the hill, not making eye contact until they were in talking distance. Somehow I knew straight away why they were there: the returned posted copyright.

I looked a fucking mess. I had my arm in plaster. I had cold sores on my lips, real scabby ones, the type that peel off like cornflakes. I also had a black eye from bashing my face on the dashboard of the car.

Edward being ever so observant says, "Hello Paul, you're looking well."

I thought, *Fuckin dick*.

I would have told him off but for Michael and Pam being there.

"What are you two doing here?" I asked.

"Well Paul, we've come to ask you if we can get the copyright off you, just in case it causes any problems in the future."

Phil just sat there looking around. He never said a word. I asked Edward what sort of problems he was on about.

"We're not really sure Paul, but just in case."

I told him that I had destroyed it. They had nothing else to say after that. I asked him why Thom hadn't come to ask for it. Edward said that Thom was really busy at uni. Edward then reminded me that there was no one at Geffen called Penny.

"No Edward – Polly, not Penny!" I snapped back at him.

They said their goodbyes and they sloped off back down the hill.

I turned to Sasha and said, "If Thom had asked for it, I would have given it to him. Edward can kiss my arse."

Michael then asked me if I still had it.

"Yes Michael, it's in Vivian's safe."

He put his hand on my shoulder, gives it a squeeze and says, "Good for you Paul. Good for you."

Clint asked me a few times if I was taking the room at his house and, at this point, I had had enough of Buckland village. It was now obvious that Thom wasn't coming back. His father and brother, Andy, came into The Lamb just before I left. They sat at the bar and I gave them their drinks. Thom's dad, with an ever-so-smug look on his face, starts telling me how well the band is doing and how fabulous the new songs are. Andy, I could see, was uncomfortable. He didn't say much. I asked him where Thom was.

His father replied, "Oh, he's in Boston having singing lessons."

I mentioned this to Thom the day that I met him on Abingdon Road. He just shook his head in disbelief.

Looking at Thom's father chomping away on the free bar nibbles and listening to him gloat was pissing me off. I went into the back room and tapped another barrel of beer just to get away from him. When I came back into the bar, they were about to leave. We said our goodbyes and as they walked out the door, I shouted to him, "Mr Yorke, I told you that they would make it."

His response was, "Yes you did Paul. Yes you did."

I really wanted to talk to Thom. I really missed him. This just added to the many reasons why I had to get out of there. I didn't even know the result from his degree. I called his parents' house, and his mother told me that he was out of the country. I never tried to get in touch again until I wrote to his father back in 2013. I had never once attempted to make contact before then.

I had really had it with Buckland at this point. I was only hanging around because of Sasha, and she had already promised that she would come with me if I left. So, with my mind made up, I called Michael and told him that the cops had been again but that I didn't open the door. I think he knew that I was lying but, being a man of his word, he told me it was time to move on.

I packed my stuff and moved into Clint's house. It was such a relief to get out of there. Besides Michael and Pam, I missed Vivian and Mr Brighton, but I couldn't be bothered about anyone else. This is where the fun and games really began.

Juxon Street is in the middle of a part of Oxford known as Jericho, hence the Jericho Tavern. When I got to Clint's I already knew what kind of house it was – it was just like the place I stayed in with the band after our night out at Downtown Manhattans, a bit scruffy and dilapidated. Most of the people who had stayed there before were students. Now Clint was renting it. Groper had the room downstairs, I was in the upstairs back room. I painted it sunshine yellow and I bought a second-hand king-size bed from a shop in Botley. Harvey and I went to collect it in his pickup truck. We looked like the Beverly Hillbillies when we pulled up outside the house.

I quickly settled in and started to create a bit of a drug round, nothing major – just enough to keep the money coming in. The house was wild – to call it a party house is an understatement. Every room was playing their own preference in dance music; you could hear five different tracks blaring out from one end of the house to the other. Clint suggested that I went to the dole office and sign on.

I could get my rent paid as well. What a result, I thought.

Now with my rent covered and a fortnightly giro coming in, all I had to do was sell drugs and party all week. I got to know every up-and-coming gangbanger during my time in Juxon Street. All they wanted was drugs. I was receiving bikes, car stereos, guitars, sound systems – anything as payment. It didn't matter to me how I got paid. I knew that I could sell these things for a bit more profit. This went on for about four months.

Clint had arranged to move into a new flat with his girlfriend. I had only moved into the house because he and Groper were there. Sasha told me that her mother had read an article about me breaking into the Outdoor Pursuit shop in Cowley, which was the truth. I stole a set of Motorola walkie talkies worth about £1,600. Sasha was so embarrassed, I promised her that I would look for a job and get out of the drug-dealing game.

I went for an interview at the Golden Lion in Wantage, and I must have still had the charm because I got the job straight away. I was made up, I just needed a place to live. I popped my head inside the launderette and asked the girl there if she knew of anyone who rented rooms.

"Yes," she says, "there's a room for rent in the shared house that I live at."

I couldn't believe it, so I went straight round to her house and asked for the landlord. This little body builder came to the door and I said, "Is your dad in?"

He replied, "My dad's dead. What do you want?"

"I'm looking for Andy."

He replied sharply, "I'm Andy."

I thought, *Shit, I've blown it here.*

I went on about the room and he invited me in. It was on the first floor and had an en-suite bathroom. I paid him £65 and moved in that night.

Sasha was still at her parents' house most nights but when she stayed over we had a great time. I wasn't selling drugs and I had started working again. We were very happy at this stage of our relationship. Now being the way that I was, I was quick to jump onto a financial opportunity. Two of the local lads, Andy and Pete, who I got to know through coming into the bar, asked me one night if I wanted to go out on the rob.

Pete said to me, "Yer Scouse, we do safes; we are a man short because Eddie had done us off for a load of TVs and video cameras."

Little did he know that I had bought this equipment off Eddie the week before and had sold it all in Oxford. Eddie was a tough little fucker – he wasn't scared of anyone. I kept my mouth shut and I agreed to go out shopping with them. "Going shopping" is how they referred to going on the rob.

My first outing with them came as a bit of a surprise. I was in bed with Sasha and the doorbell goes at about midnight. I opened it and asked them what was going on.

"Come on, Scouse. We've been out all day scouting places. We're doing two safes tonight. Hurry up and get dressed."

I ran upstairs and quickly told Sasha what was going on and that I wouldn't be too long. We were gone for about five hours. When we returned we made our way up to my room. Sasha hadn't slept. She had lain awake shitting herself.

We emptied the bags on the bed. It wasn't the biggest robbery in history, but 2,800 quid each wasn't bad for a few hours' work. We had, in our haste, also picked up sheets of folded stamps. When Pete and Andy left they didn't say anything about the stamps. I just pushed them under the bed.

About a week later I was in the post office cashing my giro and I asked the girl behind the counter if she would take the stamps. I told her that they were from my brother's business that had gone bust.

"Yes of course we do. Stamps are just like cash. How much is there?"

I wasn't sure, so I said, "About 150 quid's worth."

"Bring them in next time and I'll cash them in for you."

I went straight back to my room, got the stamps from under the bed and began to count them. I nearly shat myself when I flicked through the pages: the last few sheets were all £1 and 50p stamps. I ran back to the post office and waited until the girl had served her customer. I didn't want to go to the older woman in case she started questioning me. The girl counted out the stamps, 680 quid. I was fuckin chuffed.

I phoned Manny in Oxford and asked him to call Martin to get me a 9 bar of hash. Shit I'm drug dealing again. Once I started selling, I soon realised that there was an untapped market for hash, Es and speed. There was a famous stable close by and the jockeys there at the time became great customers. Sorry folks, got to keep the details of this bit myself.

Sasha was disappointed that I had fallen back into drug dealing, but when she saw the money coming in – and got used to the lifestyle that came with it – she soon accepted the situation.

In the meantime, I excelled at robbing safes. Almost every night of the week I was out on the make. During the day I had two young lads running around selling £5 and £10 hash deals. I would spend my evenings with Sasha, then the lads would pick me up at about midnight and off we'd go.

I was still using a pager that I got off Manny a few months before. One evening it started bleeping, so I had to walk up to the High Street to use a phone box. I needed a 20p coin to make the call but the shops were shut.

I noticed that an office still had its lights on. I knocked on the door. I couldn't believe my eyes when Thom's father appeared. I had lived in Wantage for a few months at this point. I had no idea that he had an office just doors away from where I was staying. He was just as surprised to see me. He gave me a 20p coin and we politely said our goodbyes. I lived on that street for almost a year. I made a point of always going the long way into town to avoid him. I don't know why I did that.

One night I had to go out with Sasha, so Pete and Andy went shopping without me. At around 3am they were at my door. They came upstairs with two bags of loot. One of them had a load of change in different money bags, the other contained three cotton money sacks – two of them bursting with fivers, tens and twenties. They counted out £4,000 each, that left £400, plus a bit of change. They said that I could keep it for letting them divvy up at my place. Now this other money bag, Pete put his hand inside and pulled out what he referred to as "A load of shite." In his hand were 5p, 2p, 1p, 10p and 20p coins. "Leave that," he said to Andy.

Andy says, "Scouse you might as well have that too."

Sasha's sitting there with a look of disbelief on her face. She asks me where they got the money from. I told her that I didn't know. I counted the notes and the change that they had left me. It was just under 500 quid.

"Sasha," I said, "Count how much is in that other bag."

"No, it's late, do it tomorrow."

"Just count the fuckin money!" I snapped.

"No, do it yourself!" she snapped back.

I picked up the sack and poured the money out on top of the bed making sure that most of it landed on top of the quilt she was now half hiding under. The look on Sasha's face said it all: pile after pile of brand-new, gleaming pound coins. Just the first few inches of coins were, as Pete put it, a load of shite. The rest of the bag was filled with these little golden gems.

Sasha, now beaming with excitement, says, "Shall we count it then?"

"Fuck that Sasha, we'll do it tomorrow."

Wantage was a bit of a gold mine in itself – loads of kids with loads of money to spend. My attempt at getting away from Oxford's drug scene had obviously failed. There was just as much a drug trade in Wantage as there was in Oxford Centre. I was all over the city buying drugs to sell and, as I said before, with the drugs came lots of booty. Whatever was on offer I would pay for it with drugs. I didn't like giving anyone money – not that I was tight. I just liked paying with drugs because I knew that they would only go and buy drugs if I gave them money. The way I saw it, they might as well just get the drugs off me. I would then take the stolen goods into Oxford and make even more money.

Manny called me and asked if I wanted to move back to Oxford. He was moving out of his flat behind the beauty salon in Abingdon Road. I asked Sasha, but by now she didn't care where we lived. She was along for the ride no matter what.

Before I left Wantage, a couple of wannabe drug dealers asked me if I could get them a couple of bars of hash and, as I was about to move, I agreed to buy it for them. Right from the start I had no fucking intention of buying them anything. As soon as they handed over their money, it was mine and they were getting fuck-all in return. Well, I was moving back to Oxford so the extra start-up money would come in handy.

I settled in quickly on Abingdon Road. There were loads of young people buzzing around. Manny was just around the corner and Martin was always turning up out of the blue with one scam or another, doing his best to get me involved in all kinds of shit. He was a fraudster and a drug dealer. "A little fucker" is how my Dad would have described him. Even so, we got on great. We made a few quid off one another and after I'd saved his arse with the football hooligans at the Coven, we had become good mates.

I had a good reputation in Oxford – with all the wrong kind. A couple of shop owners approached me because the local kids were hanging around their shops causing trouble. A few windows had been smashed, so I went round there with Carl Rimmer, a good friend of mine, and chased these kids off. We then later caught up with them and gave them a load of hash. They promised to stay away from, as they put it, the "Paki shops".

Now I was on good terms with the shop owners, they knew they could trust me. They bought most of the stolen goods that I was acquiring – and if I had any dodgy credit cards, they could always be relied on for a quick few quid.

Martin, now on the scene almost every day, was pestering me to move to London. He kept going on about the money that we could make. "The drug scene is well bigger in London, and we can move all the stolen goods from Oxford to London, sell it all in Loot Magazine, then do the same in Oxford with any goods that have been pinched in London."

I wasn't too keen on moving, but then Sasha got a place at the London College of Fashion. She arranged to move into a shared house with a few of her friends. For a short time, Sasha and I drifted apart. I was running around Oxford getting up to all kinds.

Manny was selling a bit of weed and a couple of local lads had tried having him off for the princely sum of 120 quid. He asked me to meet him in the Marlborough Arms on Abingdon Road. When the two lads turned up, Manny told me to wait inside while he went out and spoke to them in the car.

Manny knew that I was a bit of a hot head. I watched through the window as these fellas tried to convince Manny that they didn't owe him the money. Another lad then jumps out of the passenger door and starts threatening Manny. Manny could handle himself – I told you before that he was a six-foot taekwondo motherfucker – but these lads weren't soft either. I burst through the door out into the street giving it the big one, hand in my pocket ready to pull a blade out, my Scouse accent now overpowering everyone's conversation.

"What the fuck lad? You've had the drugs; fuckin pay for them."

These local so-called hard cases backed off straight away. Manny got his money and, again, my reputation was getting worse.

One of the nights that would cement my bad-arse reputation came the weekend after our friend died in an accident on the A34.

Toby was hit by an army truck and killed. His older brother came to the Coven nightclub with a 10-inch blade down his trousers. He hid it in the toilet. I was with him at the side of the dancefloor. It was obvious that he was agitated. He told me that he had dropped a couple of acid tablets. I had only had one drink.

While I am talking to him, this lad who had previously been fucked up in a car accident comes over to us. Now this lad wasn't too stable on his feet after the accident and he was acting a bit stupid, so Toby's older brother pushes him out of the way. This poor kid goes flying and he falls to the floor on his arse.

Within seconds about six lads come running over, looking for blood because this disabled kid had hit the ground. They surround Toby's brother and start throwing punches at him. He runs into the toilet, tripping his head off, grabs the 10-inch kitchen knife and comes running out stabbing at this lad standing by the door. I could see the blade going into his chest. It was fucking horrible.

The doorman shits himself. Everyone around shits themselves. After the third strike, the lad who was being stabbed fell back against the wall. Toby's brother, not yet finished, goes at him again. I jumped in front of him and I grabbed the hand holding the knife. I kept screaming his name so that he would know that it was me. His eyes by this stage were black and as cold as ice. He had no idea what was going on. I could tell immediately that he had well and truly lost his fuckin mind. I wrestled him towards the door, no doubt saving this kid's life because it looked as if Toby's brother was about to finish him off.

The club spilled outside and at least fifteen lads went chasing after Toby's brother, and still the bouncers did fuck all. I went back inside and shouted to the barmaid to call an ambulance. I helped the lad into a cubicle and I left him there with his friends. I knew that the cops were on their way so I jumped into a taxi and I was off.

My heroics hadn't gone unnoticed, the doorman now

seeing me take on a knife-wielding nutcase – and previously an angry football mob. My reputation as a fuckin loon was going from strength to strength.

I started going everywhere alone. I never wanted a crew around me – I always thought that that was a bit of a shitbag's way of protecting yourself. I would walk into the club with Sasha. Every time that we went there after the stabbing incident, the doorman would just say hello and back against the wall. I was never asked to pay at the Coven nightclub again. I didn't even bother to ask why they would let me come and go, I just assumed it was because they could have had a death on their hands if it wasn't for me. Also, they may have been a little embarrassed because they did fuck all to help.

Abingdon Road was a great place, the park and the playing fields just around the corner, a couple of decent pubs and, at the bottom of Edith Road, there was a rehearsal room where bands would often perform. I would sit outside smoking a joint, listening to them play. I became friendly with a lad called John. He wanted to buy a joint off me but I just rolled one and gave it to him.

Within weeks we had formed a little band, he on guitar and his mate Allen on the drums. I was doing my best Jim Morrison impression. Allen had had previous drug problems and so he was accompanied by his father everywhere he went. John had no idea that I was a full-time criminal. I gave him my normal face because I didn't want to scare him off. John was gentle and very creative just like Thom. I had learnt my lesson by now, and I was not taking shitloads of speed and Es. I had grown out of it.

One of the kids up the road from my flat stole a Rickenbacker guitar and sold it to me for 100 quid. It was worth thousands. I was too scared to move it on because I knew that it would bring unwanted attention. John, knowing that I had this guitar, comes to me with 400 quid in his hand, and like a fuckin divvy I sold it to him. Every time I see a Rickenbacker on TV my gut turns. I wish to God that I had kept it.

The band was doing okay, and then John decided to go and live in Sweden with his girlfriend the following year. Knowing that our group was now going nowhere, I stopped playing with them.

One afternoon I was using the phone box on Abingdon Road and this ginger-haired lad walks past. I looked at him.

He said, in his London accent. "What you fuckin looking at?"

I pushed the door open and said, "You, yer fuckin dickhead. Who the fuck do you think you are?"

He burst out laughing, "Ha, Ha, a fuckin Scouse. What are you doing around here, selling drugs?"

I just laughed at his bare-faced cheek. "Yer why? You got a problem with that?"

"Nope, you got anything on you now?"

Nick and I became inseparable after that. He introduced me to loads of people. There was one girl called Verity, a gorgeous little ginger nut, with the tightest curls that I had ever seen halfway down her back. A really pretty girl. I fell for her instantly but she was a bit too young for me. She was really disappointed when I pointed this out but nevertheless we became really close. It wasn't long and Verity and her friends were partying the night away in my flat. Six or seven girls, Verity, Leila, Jackie, Jo, Kelly and Clare. They were all gorgeous looking and fit as fuck. When Nick wasn't there, I was alone with all of them. We quickly became a pack. I would go out clubbing with them. The local lads would come sniffing around but as soon as they saw my ugly mug, they were off. It was great fun and the girls loved the attention.

Martin was showing up more and more and he was still going on about this move to London. Sasha was already there, so I agreed to go over and have a look around.

The next weekend I met Martin in Bethnal Green. We sat in the café on the corner and Martin went through the newspaper ads, running out to the phone box every now and then. I was getting a bit pissed off.

I was about to leave, then he said, "Just let me try this last one. It's on the Isle of Dogs, it's only around the corner."

Well, it wasn't only around the corner. We had to take the bus to get there and I fuckin hate public transport. We waited on Westferry Road for the landlord, and before I knew what was happening, Martin with his slick-talking, conman ways had me signing the fuckin contract.

Now I had two flats. This one at Knighthead Point was on the thirteenth floor, overlooking London Docklands with

Tower Bridge to the right. Even though Martin had blagged my head to get this place, I was looking forward to bringing the girls over to party the night away.

The Summer of 1994 was brilliant, all-night parties with the girls. Clint and the gang would come over to go clubbing. The drug dealing and the stolen goods, just as Martin had said, went through the roof. I still had the flat on Abingdon Road. I was reluctant to give it up, so I let my mates Dean Sinclair and Pandi P look after it while I was in London. It was great having the two places so I could come and go as I pleased.

One night Dean phones me and says, "Scouse, we came back from the pub and these four lads were trying to break into the flat. We chased them off but one of them fell over. We've got him in the flat Sellotaped to a chair. What should we do with him?"

I had just settled down with something to eat. Manny and his then girlfriend Nome had come over for the night. I told Manny what Dean had said, and made my way over to Oxford.

I was told a couple of times that the lads who I had ripped off from Wantage were out for blood, so my first instinct was that the guy Sellotaped to the chair was one of them. When I arrived, this poor cunt had been beaten up and left there for about two hours. His arms and his legs repeatedly wrapped so that there was no chance of escape. I felt a bit sorry for him when I realised that he wasn't out to get me, but at the same time it was funny as fuck.

"I'm just a burglar," he cried over and over.

He and his mates would slide people's front doors open with slices of Coke bottles. It was quite ingenious. Anyway, I unwrapped him and gave him a lift home. I never saw him again.

Next door to my flat on Abingdon Road lived a few students from Zambia in Africa. They were studying at Oxford. A few weeks before I went to London, Alex, one of the Zambian lads, tells me that his mate is bringing some weed over from Africa and he needs someone to sell it. I thought that he was full of shit but I gave him my pager number and told him to pass it on. I didn't think any more about it.

Several weeks later I was in the apartment in London, at about 11.30pm my pager starts bleeping. I had to go downstairs to the phone box and call the pager centre to retrieve the message.

The voice said, "Hey Paul, I am a friend of Alex. He told me to call you when I got here."

I phoned him back and he got a taxi straight over. It's now about 1am. The doorbell goes and there is a six-foot black lad and a skinny white kid carrying two black bin liners. The bags were obviously heavy, so I let them in and we made our way to the living room. I looked in the bag and it was kilo after kilo of weed, all broken up into large lumps. I went into the bedroom and got a large white bed sheet. I laid it on the floor and emptied the black bags out. Two big piles of weed and two massive pieces of squidgy black hash. I didn't have proper weighing scales, so I grabbed the bathroom scales. They registered at 13.5 kilos. Not accurate at all. Victor, the black lad, asks me how much he could get back on it. I knew that weed was about £2,250 a kilo, and the hash was about the same, so I just said, "About £1,400 a kilo, that's if it smokes all right."

Three of the kilos had mould on them so I told them it would be hard to sell that. Victor said I could keep it, "Just pay me for the rest."

He agreed to the price without hesitation.

Shit, I should have said a grand, I thought.

They couldn't wait to get out of my flat. I told them to call me in a week and not to be coming around all the time. They agreed that they would stay away and wait for my phone call.

The squidgy black went straight away but the weed was full of seeds so it was a bit harder to sell. I enlisted the help of Martin and Manny and, slowly but surely, the weed started to go. I had money owed to me from all over Oxford. The students were going mad for this weed. Martin was charging some of them £950 for 9 ounces, and that was bringing in just under four grand a kilo. I had money coming out my fuckin ears.

One of the local villains on the Isle of Dogs came to me one afternoon with a bar of hash.

"See what you can do with that, Scouse. It's come up from Essex. No one can sell it. You can have it for £400 a kilo."

I took the bar up to my flat and I smoked a couple of joints. I would have needed about ten spliffs to get a hit off this stuff but, even so, I knew that the students in Oxford only liked the mild buzz, so I was sure that I could sell it. Manny was now living in Lewisham and attending Goldsmiths College. I took the bar of hash over to his place and asked him if he could do anything with it.

The next few weeks, we sold it by the kilo. I had paid £400 for it, and Manny and I were selling it for £2,250. The weed and the hash were both pretty shit, but drugs were a bit scarce so people bought it no matter what, as long as they got a buzz out of it.

Carl Rimmer sold a 9 bar of weed to a group of students who lived on Chester Street in Oxford. They weren't happy with it, so they ordered another 9 ounces with the intention of taking it off him. One of them, shitting his pants, had told Carl about the set-up. I picked Verity up and we went in place of Carl. Verity was a tough little fucker but I asked her to wait in the car just in case it kicked off. I had the weed in my coat.

I stood in their kitchen and waited. I could hear them discussing their next move.

"Hey lads, come and have a look at this!" I shouted.

They didn't move. They just went quiet. Then, out of nowhere, there was a loud bang. The four-by-four piece of wood holding up their kitchen sink shattered down one side. The lad who had opened the front door to me came rushing in from the living room and he gave me 650 quid.

"I'll give the rest to Carl tomorrow."

That was the end of that. We never heard from them again.

The story of this loud bang went around as quick as shit. I became addicted to the movie, *King of New York* and I did everything that I could to be Frank White. I watched *The Krays* movie God knows how many times. People started saying that I was a gangster – was I fuck. I was playing gangster for the attention.

I got sent to Brixton Prison not long after that. I only got a three-week lie down. I realised then that I was nothing but a piece of shit, just like everyone else in there. The only difference was, Brixton was full of real gangsters. My arse fell out. (In other words, I lost my bottle).

I wasn't the cocky, full-of-himself tough guy when I came out of there. I realised straight away where I was in the pecking order, and I was nowhere near the top. Before I went to Brixton Prison I was running around London and Oxford like a fuckin loon – always because of someone causing a commotion or having a big mouth. But when I would go and see them – always alone I might add – they would shit themselves. I paid one lad a visit in the Brew House, a pub in the centre of Oxford. He had been telling people that I was after his girlfriend. I think that I said hello to her a couple of times. I walked into the Brew House and I found him sitting upstairs with another girl. I just put it on him straight away. He pulled a steak knife out of his sleeve. I put my hand inside my jacket as if I had the gun, but I didn't. If he knew that I didn't have it, I am sure that he would have stabbed the fuck out of me. He had that knife for me and no one else, plus he was game as fuck.

The story of me pulling a gun on him in the Brew House went around. No such fuckin thing but that's how gossip goes. People started paying on time, and Martin said that he was getting loads of respect from the lads in town.

Then there were these two lads I had come across through Nick, let's call them Cagney and Lacey. They were all right to get on with. One night I gave Martin two kilos of hash to sell to a lad in Oxford. I went out with Sasha, and then later that evening we made our way to Nick's house. While shooting speed, these two divvies had come up with a plan that they would grab Martin and force him to hand over whatever money or drugs he might have. I had no idea what was going on until I got to Nick's house.

Nick told me that Martin had been round looking for me, a bit shaken up, then he went on to tell me what had happened. As he's telling me this story, Cagney and Lacey turn up at the door. Nick doesn't want to let them in, not because he is scared, but because his girlfriend is six months pregnant.

I said to Nick, "These daft cunts are not going to do a thing. Let them in."

As soon as they walk in, Cagney reaches into a rucksack and I see him first pull out a Bowie knife about 8 inches in length. He puts it back into the rucksack and then he pulls out an iron bar about 12 inches long. He grabs me around the neck and he gently places this iron bar against the left side of my face. I knew right then that he didn't have the bottle.

Sasha starts screaming and then Nick's girl starts screaming her head off from the bedroom. Sasha in shock sort of climbs up the couch to get out of the way. That made me so fuckin angry. I wrestled him into the kitchen. He's at the kitchen door and I am against the sink. I quickly look around and there are knives, forks, pots and pans right next to me. I looked at Cagney and I called him on it. He froze at the door. I could have grabbed anything and smashed his fuckin face in with it. Right there I saw the balls fall out of him. Lacey is standing behind him putting on his tough-guy look.

Cagney then starts going on about how he had heard that I was out to get him, load of bollix. I decided right then that I was going to make him pay. I didn't give a shit about what he had done to me – I could cope with that – it's to be expected when you're a drug dealer. But putting it on me in front of Sasha – and knowing full well Nick's missus was pregnant? I was raging inside. But like I said before, I can hide my feelings, showing no emotion whatsoever.

The situation calmed, I asked them if they wanted a lift back to Abingdon where I knew they lived. I didn't know exactly where but I was about to find out.

Sasha protested at first saying, "There's no chance that they're getting in my car."

We drove them back to Abingdon. Cagney wanted to

stop at his sister's house first. When he got out the car Lacey's arse fell out.

"Listen, Scouse," he whinged. "All this had nothing to do with me. I didn't even know what was going on."

Cagney comes back to the car. Lacey sits back in his seat tight-lipped. We drive them to Lacey's flat. I step out of the car to let them out.

Cagney pulls the Bowie knife out and says, "Here Scouse, if you've got a problem with me, then fence me now."

I looked at the Bowie knife and I said to him, "Nar lad, just leave it."

I made my way back to Nick's and I apologised to him and his girlfriend.

As I was leaving, he asked me what I was going to do about it.

"What the fuck do you think Nick? He's getting shot."

I got back to London and I called Del, Gary and Tony, three lads who I had been knocking about with on 'the Island' (as we called the Isle of dogs). They didn't know it, but I had a replica nine-millimetre Snub Nose down my trousers.

When we left London to seek my revenge, these three were game as fuck, especially Del.

Once we arrived at Lacey's flat, his girlfriend opened the door and straight away she said, "He's in the living room".

We all stepped in and Lacey stood up in complete shock – the four of us surrounding him with his back to the couch. I pulled the gun out and I pointed it straight at his face.

As I do, Gary says, "Scouse, for fuck's sake don't shoot him."

The air was thick with emotion. Lacey fell back onto the couch, and he bursts into tears. He pulls open his shirt and he starts blabbing on about how the girl in the flat upstairs had stabbed him in the chest the night before over 10 quid. There he was, rubbing this blood-stained plaster above his left nipple, crying his eyes out. I have to tell you that this fucker is about six foot tall and a well-known street robber – he'd even rob his own mother. I had no sympathy for him at all, in fact I found the whole affair quite comical.

He went on to tell me Nick had warned Cagney that I had gone back to London to get my gun and that Cagney was now hiding out at his brother's house in Birmingham. I made Lacey come to the phone box on the corner and call Cagney. This big fucker is now trembling all the way down the street. Del, Gary and Tony are sitting in the car. They can see that this is going nowhere.

Lacey gets Cagney on the phone. I ask him where he is.

"Somewhere you can't get me," he replies.

I tell him that I'm going to sort him out, not because of what he did to me, but because he did it in front of Sasha. He tried worming his way out of it, telling me that he was off his head on speed and that he hadn't slept for days. I wasn't having it. I gave the phone back to Lacey and I stood behind him while he broke down again, telling Cagney that I had come over with the other boys from London and that I'd put a gun in his face. He kept looking over his shoulder sobbing like a child. He thought that I was going to shoot him right there in that phone box. Poor cunt. I actually felt sorry for him at this point. I told him that I wasn't after him and I calmed him down.

I am sure that was the worst night of his life, but for me it was just another night at playing gangster.

Even though I was running around Oxford and London with my replica gun, I still tried to keep my hand in the music business. I was helping the band The Blue Feilds from Oxford (You will notice that I just spelt 'Fields' wrong, tell you why in a bit). I was also working with a band from South London called Assisi. They were on the scene playing all over the capital when I got involved with them, and they were absolutely fantastic.

I remember going to see Skunk Anansie in Camden with Z, the singer from Assisi, just before Skin and the band made an impact. Z was really beautiful – tall, mixed race, outrageously sexy – and her stage performance was wild. I said before how much I hate public transport, but when I went across London with Z to the Skunk Anansie gig, she just glided her way on and off the buses. I was amazed how easy she made it look. I quickly followed her like a puppy dog follows its mother.

I was convinced that Assisi or The Blue Fields would be the Next Big Thing. I made a demo for The Blue Fields and I printed a load of posters advertising their first gig at the Marquee Club. The night that I made the demo covers and the flyers, I was stoned out of my nut and being dyslexic I spelt the Blue Fields 'Blue FEILDS'. Like a thick sod, I plastered these misspelt flyers all over the place and I sent the misspelt demo out to several record companies.

The night of the Marquee gig, I was coming down from a week of madness. When the boys finished their set, I said a few things out of place backstage in their dressing room. An American musician, who shall remain nameless in case he starts crying to his lawyers, came into the dressing room and put me in my place. That was it. Another failed attempt at managing a band. I was determined not to make the same mistake with Assisi.

Record company interest was growing, Z called a meeting at the guitarist's house over at Elephant and Castle. Just as things were starting to get going, seriously, Z sacks the guitarist and the bass player.

The first thing that the guitarist says to me is, "I suppose this is your doing?" A look of absolute contempt in his eyes.

The bass player was devastated. He couldn't believe it. He kept saying, over and over. "I gave up a job at Ronnie Scott's for this."

I felt really bad for the two of them and I was made to be the fuckin scapegoat. I wasn't having any of that, and now, having a band that consisted of a singer and a drummer, I gave up on them. At least *I* didn´t fuck this one up.

Sasha moved into her student house in Dulwich, and for a short time we again drifted apart. I was mostly with the girls at this point. I loved being with them. They would get the coach over from Oxford and we would spend the weekend getting off our heads. Verity, Leila, Jackie, Jo, Kelly and Clare – and from time to time they would bring other friends with them. I was in my element, surrounded by gorgeous girls. Losing contact with the girls has always bothered me. Out of all the relationships that I have fucked up, I can honestly say that this is one of my biggest regrets. I loved them all, just as much as I have loved any one of my partners. I hope that they all went on to have great lives.

Victor, the lad from Africa who was supplying me with weed, called me one night and said, "Scouse, I have a car, it's broken down in South London. Come over to Greenwich and get the key off me. You can have the car, just come and get it."

I couldn't believe my eyes when I got there, a Vauxhall Astra 16v, red with black skirts and BBS Alloys, black leather interior. The gasket had gone on it, so I had it fixed up at The Arches in Lime House. I thought that I was King Shit in this car.

A couple of weeks later, Martin brings his motor from Oxford and he parks it next to mine. So now parked outside our apartment is a Red Astra 16v and Martin's Red 18.i Cavalier SRI. The neighbours didn't miss a thing.

One of the fellas on the third floor asked me in the lift what I did for a living. I told him to mind his own fuckin business. This is when the shit on the estate started. I was now upsetting some of the locals for two reasons. One is that they didn't want some cocky Scouse cunt selling drugs on their patch – even though I was making money for a lot of them, I was still an outsider. But the second thing, the thing that I didn't know, was that when I'd signed the contract for this apartment, the owner had worked for the Labour Council.

When the Conservatives started selling off all the council flats, this councillor had sold out and bought the apartment. The locals were already pissed off before I had even moved in.

I quickly got a name for myself on the Island. The local lads would come round and get stoned almost every day, but when the girls came over I would only let Del in. Like I said, I loved being with the girls and I didn't want the other boys sniffing around. We were having some wild parties and the veranda outside my apartment always stunk of weed or hash. The neighbours started complaining to the council, and a couple of locals had reported me for selling drugs. I know this because when I was raided by the police for the first time, they told me that they'd had many phone calls about the parties, and the drugs were mentioned every time. Well, they found no drugs on that occasion, because when they broke the door down Verity and Leila had already smoked them all.

A few weeks later I was at my parents' house in Lancashire. Martin, having a key for the apartment. takes a load of stolen goods over in the middle of the night. He had Carl Rimmer with him and a couple of girls. The cops were called and at 4.30am they broke the door down again. I couldn't fuckin believe it. Martin was charged with handling the stolen goods and, again, I was the talk of the town.

Another night, the cops were called to an apartment a few floors below me because there was a water leak. When they went in, the whole place was full of weed plants. I got labelled with that one as well; the local gangsters asked me how much money I had lost. I didn't care what anyone said about me, it all added to the bullshit image that I was portraying, and the nightmare that was Brixton Prison soon faded into the distance. I was once again acting the twat.

One Sunday afternoon the girls went back to Oxford and I went to bed about ten. I was knackered. The next thing I know, Del and Gary are at the door with two girls. I let them in, and I went back to bed.

At six the next morning the front door is smashed off its hinges and in they come again, fuckin mob-handed this time. The CID with their armoured plod. They ransacked the place and, again, they found nothing of mine, but Gary had about two-spliffs-worth of hash on him. The copper asked me if I had a gun. It became instantly obvious that this is what they had raided me for, so someone close to me had definitely told them about the gun.

"Yes, I do. It's a replica, and it's in a box in the airing cupboard."

They sprang into action like this gun was a fuckin nuclear bomb. I kept telling them that it was a replica and that it was in bits. They arrested me and they got a ballistics team over to collect the gun. What a load of shite, they made a song and dance about fuck all. Six hours in a police cell and, when I came out, they handed the now re-organised gun back to me in a box with plastic tape over the front.

"Shit you've put it back together," I joked.

"Yes, we would like you to sign it over to us so that we

can destroy it," said one of the cops.

"Why?" I asked.

"Because we don't like little shits like you having these things lying around," came the response.

"Yer, go ahead take it. It's a piece of shit anyway."

I was still as gabby and cocky as I could be.

This being the third time that the door had been bashed in, I knew that it wouldn't be long before they got me for something – and now I was sure that someone was snitching.

I had been caught red-handed robbing the computer factory in Oxford the year before, and hadn't attended probation. I had also failed to appear on the Outdoor Pursuit shop theft – and I had a number of traffic warrants outstanding – so it wasn't going to be long before my arrest.

I was friendly with a gay couple who lived above me. They often bought a quarter of hash off me. I asked them if they wanted to store my drugs for me. In return they could smoke what they wanted, when they wanted. With this arranged, I could sleep safe. I would take a selection of VHS films to and from their apartment, each time transporting the drugs in one of the video boxes.

I wasn't raided again, but when I went to my flat on Abingdon Road in Oxford, Dean told me that the cops had been looking for me. They had been to the flat a couple of times telling him to get me to go in and see them. I knew that my time was up. The thing is, when you don't have a clue about the law, you avoid it for as long as possible, because your imagination is far worse than the outcome – in most cases anyway.

Knowing that the end was near, I was missing Sasha. Despite all the other attention that I was receiving, I wanted her back in my life. I arranged to meet her at the park in Greenwich. She looked so lovely, really tanned, long dark brown hair. She had lost a little weight making her look even more like a model than before. I was smitten. We arranged to see one another again. I started to cut my ties with everyone. I upset Verity one night after I swallowed three acid tabs. Her cassette tape of TLC got chewed up in my Sony stereo, so in a rage I snapped it in half. She left the next morning with her knickers in a twist, the others in tow.

I went back to see Sasha. She was really upset, as someone had broken in to the student house the night before and stolen their belongings. Now not feeling safe at all, she agreed to move in with me on the Island. (No, I didn´t break in, if that's what you're thinking).

I slowed right down when Sasha moved in. I was determined to get myself back on track. I got a job at Drummonds Wine Bar near Canary Wharf through the agency Reed.

In order to get paid by Reed I needed a bank account. Here I am doing my best to sort my life out and I am confronted with this unfortunate opportunity. I went to Lloyds and opened an account. They gave me a £50 guarantee card and told me that I could order a cheque book through the hole in the wall. Well, I ordered four cheque books and went around all the Bureau de Changes that I could find, cashing £50 cheques.

This was too easy. I opened another account at the Halifax telling the manager that I wasn't happy with Lloyds; another four cheque books ordered and a £50 guarantee card.

Sasha and I went shopping almost every day. I bought loads of pairs of Reebok Classics and I sold them half price to everyone I knew. Things were calming down and I was getting on with my neighbours for the first time. The wild drug-fuelled parties had stopped, and if making money was this easy, I didn't have to sell drugs.

Martin's Vauxhall Cavalier was still parked outside. One afternoon, a neighbour knocked and said, "You'd better go and have a look at your car."

Someone had popped the lock open and stolen the headlamps. *Fuckin scabs*, I thought. *Why not steal the whole car?*

Anyway, one of the fellas on the estate comes out and tells me about his mate that could fix the car, so I drove it to his garage and left it there.

About six weeks later, Sasha and I are walking in the block when this guy stops me and says, "Have you got your car back from my mate yet?"

I answered, "No, not yet."

He then said, "Are you selling drugs round here?"

That was the last thing that I remember. I came around

on the floor, the left side of my face now rearranged. It felt as if I had had a load of golf balls pushed under my skin and the left side of my jaw was bleeding.

As I am getting my head together, the lift opens and here he is again. Now I can see what he's hit me with – you know those metal things you sometimes get attached to a hotel room key – flat with a ball at the end? Well he had that clenched in his fist. That's obviously what had left the 'golf balls' all over the side of my face.

I got my head together as best I could and backed off into the street.

"Come on dickhead, get out here." I shouted at him.

At this point I didn't know that Sasha had jumped on his back, screaming at him to leave me alone. This emptied out the pub across the square, so when I got outside there was already an audience. I tried to get my head straight as he came at me. I made a desperate swing for his jaw, my fist clenched as tight as it could be. He was much taller than me and, having had the wind punched out of me not minutes before, I connected with the side of his throat. Thankfully it was enough for him to realise that I was ready for a proper scrap. He backed off and went straight inside.

I made my way upstairs. Sasha was crying her eyes out. I started laughing and I told her to stop being so silly.

"Look at your face," she said.

I looked in the mirror. I was a mess. By now the cops had had numerous phone calls about the fight. A whole gang of them turned up. They wanted me to put in a statement – but there was no chance of that. The copper told me to go to Whitechapel Hospital just to get checked out. He was convinced that my jaw was broken. I knew that it wasn't, but I went anyway.

I later found out that the guy who had attacked me was playing with a double-edged sword: he was well in with the local gangsters, making a few quid through them, but he was also a well-known informer. Anyone on the estate who he didn't like, he would make it his duty to try and get rid of them by any means. I was going nowhere, fuckin snitch.

The next winter he got his just deserts. When he was leaving his local pub, it was around six thirty in the evening and a cold, foggy night was setting in. Two lads jumped out of a car and beat the living shit out of him. They left him in a puddle of piss and have a guess who got the blame for that?

The Oxford cops had been, again and again, to the flat on Abingdon Road. I told Sasha that I was going to get it sorted out. I arranged with the custody sergeant that I would come in and face the music. He promised me that he would do his best to get me bail, and that if I surrendered, there would be more chance that the CPS would allow it.

Sasha dropped me off. I told her that I might not see her for a while but not to worry. I was early arriving at the police station. After being processed I was then taken straight across the road to the Magistrates' court. I was granted bail and I was ordered to attend probation. I asked that the case be transferred to London. Big mistake, because when I missed court, the coppers at Lime House Police Station were all too happy to come and arrest me. As I mentioned earlier, I was given a three-week lie down in Brixton Prison. They used to call it a short, sharp, shock. Fuck me, did it work. I was instantly put in my place. I went into the shower the first day that I arrived. Some old fella came in, squatted down beside me, and pulled a bag out of his arse and he washed it right next to me. Six or seven lads came in and he dished out whatever it was. They quickly left and the old fella pushed the bag back up his arse. That was it. I had a strip wash in my cell every day after that. I thought, *Fuck that for a game of soldiers.*

Thankfully, the judge on my next appearance let me out on the proviso that I attended probation at the Mile End office. I tell you, I didn't miss an appointment.

Del, one of the lads who I had got to know on the estate where I was living, was at college. When he got off the bus around three, instead of trekking all the way up to the thirteenth floor he would shout up from the square below. My balcony door was always open during the day, and everyone who came to see me did that.

One afternoon, Del shouts up, "Scouse, you in there?"

I stepped on to the balcony, looked over and shouted back, "Yer, come on up."

A few moments later I opened the door to see a look of surprise and confusion on his face.

"What's wrong with you?" I asked.

"Scouse you're not gonna believe it, but when I shouted up to you and you looked over the balcony, some fella sitting in a car had a long-lensed camera. He pointed it up towards you and he started taking pictures."

I wasn't sure whether or not to believe him, so I just replied with, "It's probably the coppers, you know that they're after me."

The next morning Sasha left for college. It was around ten thirty. I was sitting in front of the TV, when there was a knock at the front door. I quickly turned the TV off and just sat for a few seconds in silence. Another knock. I still didn't move, then a voice shouts through the letter box.

"Paul, Paul McCarthy, I'm not a policeman. I am not here to arrest you. I'm from Victim Support. I'm here to see if you're okay."

I had just been bashed around the head, so I accepted what he said and let him in. He came in wearing a T-shirt and a faded blue pair of jeans. His hair was grey, I would say that he was about fifty. I was still in my dressing gown. I asked him if he wanted a drink but he declined. He sat at the end of the sofa. I sat in the armchair under the double glass window that overlooks the balcony. This is how the conversation went:

"So, Paul, I heard that you had a fight the other night and you got a little beaten up."

"Yer, just some local fella thinking he's a bit tasty – nothing to worry about. So why are you here?"

"Well, like I say, I'm just here to see if you're okay, that's all, and to ask if you are worried about anything?"

"No mate. I'm okay."

"You're not from around here?"

"No, I'm from Liverpool, but I've just recently moved over from Oxford. Things have been a bit crazy since I got here."

"Things, what things?"

"Well, I've been raided by the police three times. They only came once for me though. The other two times it was for my mate Martin."

The kettle had boiled itself off so I got up to go to the kitchen. As I stood up my dressing gown came slightly undone.

I turned to my right and re-tied the belt around my waist. As I turned back towards him, he had a small silver thing in his hand, about the size of a ten-pack of cigarettes.

I asked him, "What's that?"

"Oh, it's a camera," he replied.

He placed it on the end of the coffee table in front of him.

"Did you just take a picture of me?" I asked him.

"No Paul. No, I did bring it to take pictures of your injuries, but you don't seem to have any."

"I've just got a little cut on my chin, nothing to worry about," I replied.

I went into the kitchen to make a cup of coffee. He got up and made his excuses to leave, shook my hand and wished me good luck.

I told you at the start of this story that I hadn't listened to much of Radiohead's music since the release of their second album *The Bends* – and this is why: The tracks *Fake Plastic Trees, My Iron Lung, Street Spirit (Fade Out), The Bends, High and Dry* and *Black Star* had taken their toll on me, but track seven, *Just,* and how Thom got the information contained in that track....

> ...*Hanging out the fifteenth floor*
> *You've changed the locks three times*
> *He still comes reeling through the door*
> ...*You do it to yourself you do*
> *And that's what really hurts*
> *You do it to yourself*

Ok, so it was the thirteenth floor – but how on earth did he get these details if not from the little sneak who sat on my couch? How did the picture taken by the sneaky little fucker of me standing in front of the double-paned window, overlooking my balcony, end up on the inlay of the album *The Bends*?

This shit absolutely freaked me out, yet I didn't notice the photo until much later, when I was driving through France in 2003. It was the artwork within the inlay of *OK Computer* that made me look again.

Soon, I will give you an insight into the track *The Tourist*, off the album *OK Computer* – and how the Canary Wharf sketch on the inlay of *The Bends* helped set me on this journey to write my autobiography. In my mind I thought, *There is no way, Thom, that you are getting away with this.*

Untouchable

Paul McCarthy

Camara

While I was in prison at HMP The Mount, I wrote and recorded a song called *Untouchable* and sent it to Factory Fast Records in New York. They released it on this promotional album *Camara* (above) back in 2016. The track was my response to Thom running like a frightened child to his lawyers Statham Gill Davies – "Oh protect me from this monster, please!" Silly sod. You can hear it on Spotify, where I go under the artist name 'Gangster Troll'.

I still had weed and hash being sold in Oxford, so I would go there once or twice a week. The weekend after my visit from the so-called Victim Support worker, I made my way over there.

One of the lads I knew who worked on the door at the Brew House asked me if I could get some cocaine. He told me that everyone was looking for it, but no one seemed to be able to get it.

Just as a tester I bought 10 grams off my mate Ronnie, and made my way to Oxford on the coach. This coke was really strong. At this time in my life, coke didn't interest me, but I had had a line of it the night before just to make sure that it was right. I had a load of teething powder at my flat on Abingdon Road, so my intention was to make it to my flat without being stopped by the police and cut the 10 grams into 20, therefore maximising my profits and, seeing as no one had coke I knew that it would be easy to sell. Ten grams of coke would most definitely have gotten me a few nights in the cells at Saint Aldgate's nick, so I didn't hang about.

When I got off the coach in the city centre, I began walking up Abingdon Road as fast as I could. I had just been beaten up, so I was more focused on people coming up behind me than in front of me. I thought the cops were taking pictures of me, and I was stoned, so to say that I was paranoid is an understatement.

Then just like that, there he is, standing at the bus stop right in front of me, looking directly at me. As I made my way towards him, I was surprised that he was there.

Many times, in the press it has been reported that the track *The Tourist*, off the album *OK Computer*, was written about a guy who Thom came across while on holiday in Paris.

I can assure you that this account is absolute nonsense. I am now going to relay the conversation that we had at that bus stop, together with some of the lyrics that subsequently appear on *The Tourist*, and you can form your own opinion on the matter:

"Thom, hello mate. Shit, what are you doing here? Where are you going?"

> *It barks at no one else but me.*
> *Like it's seen a ghost.*
> *They ask me where the hell I'm going...*

He wasn't surprised to see me at all.

"Oh, I'm just going into town. How are you?"

I was far from fine. I was paranoid as fuck walking up Abingdon Road.

"I'm fine Thom. I'm just here for the night – 'the tourist'. I live in London by Canary Wharf now."

As mentioned, within the inlay of *The Bends*, Thom has a sketch of Canary Wharf along with the text "**I AM CANARY WHARF**".

I went on to tell him about my last meeting with his father, back at The Lamb.

"Your dad told me that you were in Boston having singing lessons. I knew that you would make it, Thom."

He shook his head slightly in disbelief. I looked over my

left shoulder. There was a car parked right on the junction of Edith Road which got my back up a bit. Thom looking at me in this way, I said to him.

"You've changed, Thom."

He replied, "No, I haven't Paul."

The Thom now standing in front of me was clean shaven with long bleached-blonde hair. Sally at Mahogany had told me that she was the one who did his hair. He was dressed in smart new clothes and here he is telling me that he hadn't changed. He was just a little skin-headed scruff when I last saw him.

I said that I had to get going. The car parked on Edith Road was giving me the creeps anyway. We said our goodbyes, and I quickly made my way along Abingdon Road.

Hey man slow down, idiot slow down.

I wasn't an idiot when I was handing over my fuckin money.

I soon reached my flat. I looked back but he was long gone.

It barks at no one else but me
Like it's seen a ghost
They ask me where the hell I'm going at
a thousand feet per second
Hey man slow down... idiot slow down.

A lost guy who Thom came across in Paris? I might have been lost in a world of drugs but I hadn't lost my memory.

I often wish I had paid more attention to the song *Thinking About You*, from the album *Pablo Honey*, before this Abingdon Road encounter. It seems obvious to me now that Thom was fighting his own feelings as to whether or not he should still be in contact with me. If I had listened more closely before I bumped into Thom that day, maybe my reaction to seeing him again would have ended a little more constructively.

When I look at all the things that Thom has used and referred to in relation to my life and our time together, I have often wondered if, in a way, he's doing all this to push me into doing something about it.

"Come on Paul, for fuck's sake, fight back! I've laid it all out before you, wake up and fight!"

Maybe I am delusional.

A few days later, I was on the train going back to London after collecting three kilos of weed in Oxford. When I got to Didcot Parkway Train Station, the announcer came over the Tannoy and informed us that, due to a technical problem, we had to change trains. As I made my way through the underpass to get to the next platform, again I couldn't believe my eyes. I am on the left side of the underpass and to my right, walking in the same direction are Edward O'Brien and producer David Smith.

"Hello Edward," I said. "How are you?"

"I'm okay, Paul. How are you?"

"I'm fine. I saw Thom the other day."

"I know Paul, he told me."

We literally had seconds to talk. I looked at him. He had had his long hair cut off, nice and short. He was dressed in what looked like new clothes. My parting comment was –and I said this on purpose – "You've changed Edward."

"No, I haven't Paul. No I haven't"

I grinned as I walked up the stairs to the left. They both walked up the right-side staircase.

If you care to take a look at the inlay of *OK Computer*, you will see a dissected railway station with three figures in the underpass. If you look closely at the figure on the left you may, or you may not see what I see.

When I bumped into Edward and David, I had a large holdall hanging off my right shoulder. This contained the three kilos of weed and a load of my clothes. Funny how this little figure in the underpass looks like it's carrying something over his shoulder.

The things I have just mentioned all happened within weeks of one another: the long-lensed camera, the Victim Support worker, the meetings with Thom and Edward. Coincidence? Oh shit, there's that word again. I'm convinced that the little man who had tricked his way into my apartment was a private detective hired by Thom to track me down.

The lyrics to the track *Creep* really do fit here. Whether they were written about me or Thom, it makes little difference.

When I realised what he had been up to with his weird spying tactics, I decided that the song belongs to him.

They brought in the C.I.A.
The tanks and the whole marines
To blow me away
To blow me sky high

There is no doubt in my mind that these lyrics – from the track *The Bends* – are a direct reference to the detective agency that Thom enlisted to spy on me. **(Note to Thom's lawyers: ask Thom, and then call me a liar. I dare you).**

London was becoming a bit too much. After the fight with the fella and his metal cosh, things just wouldn't let up. The local British National Party (BNP) still had a grievance with my landlord over the property thing that I mentioned.

I woke up one morning, and pushed inside my letter box was a death threat from someone claiming to be the BNP. I don't know if it was a real threat or just some divvy on the estate acting up. On the paper was a picture, hand-drawn of a grave with my name on it – '**Paul McCarthy, Rest In Pieces**'. On the side of the grave were two knives covered in blood.

I called my landlord and she turned up an hour later with the C.I.D from Lime House Police Station. Funny thing was, this copper made a comment about tearing off cheques and leaving fingerprints – about how it's hard to get prints off paper but much easier to get them off cheques. I was sure this was a reference to my cheque swindling.

It was time that I left London. Things were becoming a bit tasty, and I was sure that my next move was either hospital or prison and I didn't fancy either.

Sasha went to stay with her sister, and I made my way back home to Skelmersdale. I walked out of the apartment with a bag of clothes. I left everything behind. Whenever I split, I leave as much negative energy behind as I can and that includes material things. Anything that reminds me of a bad moment in my life gets fucked right off – I always start again.

I rented a small flat from my mate and I went into hiding

for a short time. I sat in the flat drinking and taking drugs for a few months. I piled the weight on.

As soon as the flat was redecorated, Sasha came to live with me again. We settled in and I started going to the gym with my mate Tony. He was a Sted Head (steroid user) and I decided to give it a go. Performance enhancers are great for getting in shape. I wasn't interested in being a monster like the other body builders – I just wanted to get fit, but the steroids that I was taking quickly took hold and I ended up weighing sixteen and a half stone. I had a fat belly, but I was as strong as an Ox.

With the steroids came the sun beds. I was looking good and Sasha and I had a great time in Skelmersdale. Before long, I had my fingers in a few pies. I got a job at Manchester Airport and I was also selling cocaine on the side.

Then, out of the blue I got a job offer in Germany. Believe it or not I really hated the situation that I had put myself in, selling drugs all the time and getting high. It really wasn't me. No matter what you might think, even with these crazy past few years, I was a worker. I always have been. Mum and Dad taught us to get off our arses and earn a living. I had worked since I was fifteen – well since I was six if you count the summer jobs and the paper rounds that I had.

I was now desperate to get out of the mess that I had created for myself. I jumped at the chance to go to Germany and, within a week, Sasha was at her mother's house and I was on a flight to Berlin.

How to Disappear Completely – track 4 from the album *Kid A*, released in 2000. I have a funny feeling that word 'coincidence' is about to make yet another appearance.

One of my brother's mates met me at Tegel Airport and took me back to his house. He told me that we were not staying in Germany, and that we were going to Holland the next morning.

We drove from East Berlin to Venray in Holland the next day. We met an agent who told us to be on site the next morning. I was to be a carpenter's mate.

We went for a drink in Venray town centre.

I noticed in a shop window that there was a sale on Fender and Epiphone guitars. With my first month's wages, I bought a Fender Telecaster Slimline and a black Les Paul-style Epiphone. I was still convinced that I could achieve something through music.

The first pub that we went into gave us directions to a bed and breakfast, a little house in the village of Wervslo. We settled in and we got to work. I was so surprised how easy it was to come off drugs and get my head together.

Within weeks Sasha was with me. We spent the summer of 1997 in absolute bliss.

No Radiohead, no drugs (even though the album *OK Computer* was released around this time, I had made a conscious effort not to think about Thom). I was back on track and fitter than ever. Sasha was back and forth all the time. She had a job at Zara in Oxford, so she didn't move out to Holland full time but, even so, our relationship seemed stronger than ever.

One afternoon she called me and said, "You're not going to believe who came into the shop today."

I was messing around and I said, "I dunno, the Pope?"

"No, Thom. Thom Yorke. He came in to pick up some clothes for his girlfriend. I know her from the shop. I didn't realise that she was with him."

I wanted to know if he had asked after me, but Sasha said that she didn't talk to him – she just looked at him and smiled. He smiled back and then walked out. She later told me that she never saw his girlfriend in the shop after that.

A few months earlier, Thom had walked into the Little Chef on the A420 where Sasha was working, prior to her getting the job at Zara. She told me that he came in to use the phone. Again, he had smiled at her but didn't say a word. Even then I was still hoping that he would want to see me, and I was a bit miffed that he didn't ask about me – sad fuck, wasn't I?

I was on the roof at Shell in Rotterdam fixing some steal sheets. There was a guy standing at the top of the ladder shouting in a cockney accent.

"Oi, are you Paul? Oi are you Paul?"

This six-foot, cockney wide boy walks over. "Aw Wight, my name's Gazza, are you Paul?"

"Yer mate, have the agency sent you?"

"Fuck me," he says. "You're a fuckin Scouser."

I replied in the best cockney accent I could. "Fuck me, you're a fuckin cockney."

We both started laughing and after that first meeting, we quickly became friends. Gary was so fuckin funny, such a laugh to be around. We started going out drinking together and before long the inevitable happened.

"Paul you want a line of this?"

Fuck, balls, arse and all the other stupid fuckin swear words combined – I said yes.

Just like that I started using again – only this time it was straight-up, class-A cocaine. I was in Holland, it had to be.

Before long I was involved again, people from the UK asking me could I get things in Holland, and the lads who I met in Holland asking could I sell things in England. Gary and I had soon set up our first deal. This would continue for a few years.

I would love to tell you more about our escapades, but Gary is not with us anymore. I think that it's unfair to talk about him in this way. Just know this: he was staunch, hard as fuckin nails and he didn't suffer fools lightly.

Gary was gone and I continued to work on the sites but my sideline was still dealing, drinking and taking drugs. That could only lead one way: down.

It wasn't long, and I was back in the UK. I had been on the waiting list at the council in Skelmersdale for an apartment. When I returned from Holland, I was given a maisonette. I decorated it and I bought all new furniture and fittings. Sasha moved in with me straight away.

It's now mid-2000, we were still very much in love, despite the fact that Sasha had only ever told me she loved me once, and that was under duress. She just couldn't show her emotions like that. Sometimes I thought she would follow me to the ends of the earth and then, other times, I felt like nothing more than a stepping stone. I would convince myself that she was just waiting to fuck off with the next best thing. This is no doubt directly connected to my inability to trust anyone.

The drugs still fuelling me, I became a little more paranoid and depressed at being back in England. I started working with a lad from Liverpool, moving a bit of stuff around the country. I was now snorting shitloads of coke every day. My mate suggested that I smoke the shit instead.

He said, "You're always blowing your nose and you look fucked. I just smoke one an evening, and then I take a Valium to get my head down."

I told him that I was concerned about smoking crack and about how addictive it was.

He just laughed at me and said, "For fuck's sake – you're addicted to coke anyway. What difference will it make?"

I thought about this over the next few days and I really did look a fuckin mess. I was putting on weight again, or should I say, I was bloated due to all the drugs that I was putting up my nose. I asked him how to make crack, and for the next year and a half I got deeper and deeper into it.

At first it was okay, I had stopped snorting during the day. I would do whatever I had to and, when I got back, I would cook a couple of grams, smoke that, then get my head down after taking a couple of diazepam. Out of my nut, I would eat like a pig. By mid-2002, I was just under seventeen stone, fat as a fuck – I even got the nick name 'Fat Paul', which really pissed me off.

Sasha and I were not getting on at all. She started staying at her mate's house in Manchester on weekends. I didn't care. I was left alone with my crack pipe. I was now in love with it.

I became more and more paranoid and anxious. I convinced myself that Sasha was cheating on me.

One morning, I drove her to Wigan station, so that she could catch the train to Manchester. There was a lad standing out front.

She looked at him and then she looked back at me and said, "I'm not kissing you goodbye."

"Well fuck off out of the car then." I snapped. Even then, I just wanted her out of the way so that I could get back home and cook a couple of grams.

I knew that we were falling apart and that it was all my fault. She never did anything to hurt me. I was just a selfish prick feeling sorry for himself for throwing his life down the toilet.

I tried reaching out to her a few times – I really needed help – but I think by now she had had enough of me. I thought that there was no hope left and I quickly fell deeper and deeper into a fucked-up depression. I could turn on the charm one minute, and the next I would be ready to fuckin kill someone. I never felt like killing myself, but I can tell you that I wanted to die. This feeling hadn't just started; I had felt like this since I was a kid.

I smoked so much crack one night that my whole body felt like it was lifting off the chair. From my toes to the tips of my fingers were vibrations like pins and needles, up my spine and through my body.

My legs lifted off the ground and I began twitching violently. After about a minute of this I collapsed onto the floor and began to sweat. The sweat was completely out of control, I had never had this happen before.

I lay on the floor waiting for my body to shut down. I was convinced that this was the end. I kept saying it in my mind and, do you know what? I didn't care. I was just waiting to die. I was content.

This event soon passed. I went down to my kitchen and cooked yet another couple of grams. I would put myself in harm's way just to prove a point – like I always had. If any of the kids at school dared me to do anything, I would do it, fuck the consequences.

I just wanted to get it over with. I would sit in the back bedroom and smoke for two days straight. Sasha never said a word, and I was truly convinced that she didn't give a shit about me anymore.

I smoked so much one night that I had a mental breakdown. Sasha called my brother Andy. He came over at six in the morning. I was still in the back bedroom afraid to come out. I asked him was there a helicopter over the house looking for me.

He started laughing and said, "You cracked cunt, it's the fuckin central heating."

He took the last of my crack off me and flushed it down the toilet promising to come back and get me later. I took a couple of Valium and I tried to sleep. It was no use; my head was fucked.

Sasha had gone to work and, knowing that Andy was coming back, I couldn't stop thinking about what the day would bring. He came and collected me. We drove to the Piper Clinic in Manchester. That afternoon I was in Rehab.

I cried for the first two hours, sobbing like a fuckin baby. My case worker slowly brought me back to reality and, over the next few weeks, she repeatedly stuck metal studs in my ears (an acupuncture stress remedy, apparently) and she talked and talked and talked.

One thing she kept telling me was to face up to things,

and to deal with the negatives around me, one by one.

In my fuckin stupor, I told myself that Sasha was the biggest negative I had, which, when I think back now, I know was ridiculous – but she was the only thing that connected me to Buckland Village and, along with all the Radiohead bollocks, I decided that she had to go.

Once I was out of rehab, I packed her belongings and took her to her father's house in Oxford. As I was leaving, she put her arms around me, and she tried to give me a kiss. She hadn't kissed me for over a year.

I pushed her away and said, "It's too late for that."

Even then she didn't put up a fight. She just accepted what was happening, with not a word.

I knew that I had done the right thing. I was killing her as well as myself. Even now I miss her almost every day.

When I told my mother what I had done, she said, "You've always been a heartless little bastard. She was a lovely girl."

JUST

I was going to call this book *Buckland Road* – the setting of my *'Subterranean Homesick Alien'* encounter. When I turned right off the A420 that day, my life took a turn for the worst.

The original sign for The Lamb has long gone, but this signpost has been here for years. Maybe in hindsight I should have kept driving.

The beginning of my recovery
(Well, almost)

Not long after I came out of rehab, a guy I had known for many years came to see me out of the blue one night. He had an issue with some Turkish fellas. I agreed to help him and, the following week, I was in Istanbul. This came just before I broke up with Sasha. Here I was on the other side of the world, and I had left her without so much as an excuse. I was on a boat going across the Marmaris Sea, thinking, *What the fuck have I done?*

There was no way that I was getting any coke out here. I just sat there thinking about Sasha, feeling sad. I called my mother and, while I was talking to her, this Turkish fella who my mate was having trouble with started throwing peanuts at me.

I fuckin lost it.

I threatened to throw this cunt overboard. I remember thinking, *I don't know what my mate is so worried about*, as this Turk bursts into tears, whinging like a fuckin fanny in front of everyone.

My mate calmed the situation down. I was the bad guy again – but that's why he brought me along: to let this prick know that there would be no fucking about.

We arrived back in England, and my mate realised that I could be quite useful. He gave me a job and, before I knew it,

I was only snorting a bit of coke at the weekends. That trip to Turkey had done me the world of good.

A week in the sun after my three weeks of therapy sorted me right out. I straightened up and I got on with the business of making money – and how I made that money made no fucking difference to me whatsoever.

I began moving around from firm to firm, making loads of connections. Because I had contacts in Holland, I climbed the ladder pretty quickly. I started moving things all over Europe, small things to begin with. A hundred keys of pot from here to there, ten keys of coke down to this place or up to that place. This was when I returned home and got slapped in the face with the album *Hail to The Thief*.

I went out and I bought the CD, along with *OK Computer*. They were the only two Radiohead albums in the shop or I would have bought the others, too. I knew at this point that I was going to fight back. I had spent too much time feeling sorry for myself.

I had made a shitload of mistakes in my life up to this point; I was determined that I wouldn't make another.

I shared the driving duties at this time with another lad who I had got to know. When it was his turn to drive, I would listen to every word that Thom said in every song.

I was driving through Spain one afternoon and I began to wonder if Thom thought that I was dead, or maybe so incapacitated due to my drug use that I had lost my memory. He knew how important my poetry was to me. He was also fully aware that I had spent months reciting my work to anyone who cared to listen. Surely he knew in his heart that I would recognise my lyrics, my poetry and songs?

I began to seriously question his motives. I know that I have mentioned this before, but this notion that he was trying in some way to goad me into action, played and played on my mind for years.

My mate would cringe when I told him about this song and that song, these lyrics and those lyrics. It wasn't fair to put him through it anymore, so I bought a Sony CD Walkman, and before long I could sing the whole album word for word without missing a beat. I would often catch him turning the radio off to listen to me.

"Fuckin dickhead," he would say, with a big grin on his face.

I was still fat as fuck, but I was clean – well, apart from the odd line up my nose.

Because our crack fiend had gone missing, me and my mate had to go to Rome to see someone. I popped a couple of Es when our freight train left Freiburg in Germany. We were going through the Alps at two miles an hour. When the sun came up at 5.30am, I was sitting next to the window rushing my tits off. What a sight. My first time travelling through the Alps, and I felt like I did it in style, even if I was in a smelly-arsed train.

We had a good few quid on us, so we decided to stay for a few days. We went to a five-star hotel just off the Piazza del Colosseo. My mate was like Ian Rush, tall and dark, he looked just like a sportsman. The staff at the hotel thought that we were working for one of the football teams in Rome. We just went along with it. There was no need for them to think otherwise.

We bought some clothes that afternoon. I purchased a lovely white-cotton shirt and, even though I was a fat fuck, I felt good in it. We went out that evening and sat on a terrace outside one of the restaurants. Our food arrived and, from across the street, came a group of young women. One of them caught my eye and she smiled at me. I smiled back and her friends giggled at her for flirting.

My mate, never one to miss a trick, says to me, "Before you go near something like that, you want to go and take a long, good look in a fuckin mirror."

What he said wounded me, but he was right. I was in a fucking state. I still had a couple of blood-filled cysts on the top of my head and I was fat and greasy. I sat there eating a T-bone steak, telling myself to enjoy it because it was going to be the last.

When I arrived back in England, I went to town and bought the revised edition of Dr Atkins' diet book. Several doctors in the States had looked at the diet again and had come to the conclusion that, in moderation, it could actually be less dangerous than first reported.

On my next trip to Spain, I read the book, and then I started to read it all over again on my way back to the UK. By the time I got home, I had memorised everything that I could eat and all the shit that I couldn't. I looked in every mirror I could find, just like my mate had said.

My next addiction became diet and exercise. When I was in the UK, I would go to Edge Hill College and run their track in the pitch-dark of night so that no one would see my tits wobbling up and down. I was ruined physically, and my mental health wasn't in a good way, but that comment kept pushing me on.

> ... *Take a good look in a mirror*
> *Take a good look in a mirror...*

I was soon given a helping hand with the diet – but not in a way that I would recommend to anyone. I was given the task of collecting a container full of furniture from a French port. I had no idea it was full of cigarettes, HONEST. Anyway, the French customs were all over it. I drove this furniture up past Calais towards the Belgium border and, sure enough, they surrounded me, the armed police in their shitty little cars. I didn't know this, but they had looked in the container when it was sent from China. They had established that it wasn't furniture so they decided to let it go and see what stupid fuck picked it up. That stupid fuck just happened to be me.

I ended up on remand in Maison d'Arret de Loos, the worst shithole of a prison that anyone had the bad fortune of being sent to. It was a fucking stinking dump and they absolutely hated my English fuckin guts. If it wasn't the French guards giving me shit, it was the French Algerian kids, who would have loved to have smashed my head in, just because I spoke English, nothing more.

I met a Scouse lad in there, and he got me on the football team. Mick had been in Loos for years on drug charges. I had no idea what the fuck was going on. Thankfully Mick was a bit of a hardcase and the French lads respected him. I wasn't alone anymore, and I soon settled in.

Mick had me out every morning in the yard doing football-style training. I was sticking to my diet, not a gram of shit went down my throat – and if I did lose faith and eat a packet of cookies or a bar of chocolate, I would put my fingers down my throat and spew it back up.

Bulimia got hold of me just as quick as the crack did. I am still fighting bulimia.

If you don't know how it affects you, it goes something like this: If I bought a chocolate cake, enough for eight people, I would have a slice and, even while I'm eating it, I already know that I am going to throw it back up. This is because I'm feeling so guilty, while at the same time, I am enjoying every mouthful, knowing that I'm going to throw it up. Now, with that delicious enjoyment that I'm feeling, in a split second, I decide to eat every last piece of this chocolate cake like a fuckin pig, devouring it in such a disgusting manner. I sometimes giggle and laugh hysterically in the midst of a full mouth. The cake gone, I am still in a feeding frenzy. Now I have two choices: continue to waste whatever food I have in the fridge, or go to the toilet and shove my fingers down my throat. The fingers always win. If I have trouble getting anything back up, I drink a couple of litres of warm tap water, lay on my back and swish my stomach contents back and forth. A couple of minutes of this and I am puking a chocolate fountain. Do not try this at home – or anywhere else for that matter.

It was also in Loos that I tried to write my memoirs for the first time, going over Radiohead's music and doing my best to write down what I was thinking. I was doing okay. Every night in my cell I would concentrate on my story. It came out all over the place at first, in fragments. I would then sit for hours putting it all into perspective. It's the only thing that I left that prison with, apart from the clothes on my back. I got up to 55 pages – not a lot I know – but it was a start, and for me it was the hardest thing in the world.

This was my first attempt.

Every day in Maison d'Arret de shithole was a challenge. It was as if you were in a war zone and you had to continuously maintain a certain level of madness in order to cope. I heard one lad getting his head bashed in with a wooden stool one night. His cell mate did it to him. The horrendous screams came down the wing… aaarrrggghhh THUD, aaarrrggghhh THUD, AAARRRGGGHHH THUD. The screams finally stopped but the thuds just kept on.

For what seemed like an age, the whole wing was in silence, as if an electric charge had been spread from cell to cell. I heard the guards running down the wing and then everyone started banging on the doors and shouting at the top of their voices. I put my hands over my ears. The noise was so bad, I thought that I was in a mad house. The whole place was on lockdown while they pulled this nutter out and scraped up the body off his cell floor.

I was released after five and a half months. The barrister pointed out that the seal on the container was the very same seal that the French customs officer had put on while it was in China, so how could I possibly have known what was in it?

I was released that day. Now I was twelve stone, with a 28-inch waist and fit as a butcher's dog. The only problem was that, along with the mental problems I had prior to going into prison, I had come out with my head up my arse. I was still in the war zone.

When I arrived back in England, my brother left me alone in his house with a cupboard and a fridge full of booze. I sat in the kitchen and did my best to drink everything that there was. I wanted coke so, smashed out of my head, I took his wife's car, drove down Stannanought Road, which is about one mile in length, and kept my foot to the floor until the road ran out. I crossed another road doing about 85mph and hit a road sign, smashing it to pieces. I went flying through the air and crashed in the middle of the roundabout. I couldn't believe it; I didn't have a scratch.

The car was barely driving. I reversed off the roundabout and drove around town until I was rescued by my cousin

Dave. He took me to his mate's house so that the cops didn't find me. How I didn't die that day I'll never know.

I ended up on anti-depression medication and my brothers supervised my recovery. My mates Brian and Dave stayed with me constantly for two weeks until I was mentally strong enough to get on with things. Phew. Thank the fuck that's over. Writing this section has absolutely drained me.

I again began to train every night at Edge Hill College, and once word got out that I was back on track, I was back in Europe doing what I did best.

First, I had to get rid of my memoirs. If I was going back into criminality, I wouldn't want anyone getting hold of them. The way I saw it, there was no point in being asked any unnecessary questions. I burnt them in my mate's garden.

After a little while, I started going back to Holland to see my mates. I had not been there long when I started seeing a Dutch girl. Things went all right at first but I soon got fed up with her constant fuckin whining. I thought that I had issues, but this thing, as lovely as it was, had a head as mad as a box of frogs. She couldn't keep her knickers on for five minutes, and I don't mean that she was taking them off for me. I stood in a shop with her one night and behind my back she's making hand signals to some fella.

I took her to England to meet my son Peter, who was studying at Stafford University. We stayed over for the weekend. Peter had told his mate Chris about my involvement with different bands over the years. Chris gave me his demo tape and I promised him that I would see what I could do.

When I arrived back in Holland, my business was taking off. I had little time for myself. Chris's demo was put on a shelf with a few others.

A couple of months later, Peter calls and tells me that Chris's song has been picked up by DJ Tiesto and that Chris is in Holland recording. I was made up for him.

A fortnight later Chris sent me two VIP tickets for his first performance at the Jaarbeurs Theatre in Utrecht – 10,000 Dutch kids going nuts. The Dutch really know how to party. As Chris makes his way on stage, I am standing with my son and Chris's girlfriend. The girl who I was with had disappeared. I was engaged in Chris's performance so I didn't see what was going on behind me.

Peter pulls my arm and says, "Dad, what's going on over there?"

I turned to look and there was my so-called girlfriend making advances towards one of the Radio 538 DJs. She had no idea that we were watching her.

I just said to Peter, "It's all over for her mate."

I used her for a place to stay after that. As soon as I found my own place, I fucked her off. She cried her eyes out, screaming down the hall WWWWHHHHHYYYYYY!

I decided that girls were out the window for the time being, relationships anyway.

I was given an opportunity to work for an agent on the building sites, in and around The Hague. While I was in Holland, my mate had gone off to do his own thing with some girl who he had met in Amsterdam. It's now 2005 and without knowing it I was about to go legit for the first time in years.

I was working as a window fitter on a job in Utrecht, just for a couple of weeks, and the Dutch lad who I was working for asked me if I knew any other English guys like myself who didn't mind putting the work in. I contacted my Scottish mate Robert and he started working for me as a subcontractor. Another lad then came, then another. After that a company in Rotterdam asked for a couple of people, then a company in Zwolle, and before I knew it, by 2007 I had twelve lads working all over Holland.

Things just got better and better. I was training every night. I had a tan all year round. I was spending time on the northwest coast of Italy. Money again was flowing with ease and I was enjoying spending it. I had a wardrobe full of dark jeans and black shirts, this would later be known as my uniform. From Tommy Hilfiger to Armani, I had a great collection, and I'd bought about ten different bottles of aftershave. I had never been a ponce and now I was full of myself, forty years of age and I didn't have a care in the world.

That year I had a few short-term relationships, some good, some bad. One in particular had wounded me before I had a chance to break it off, which was by now the norm for me. Before I got too close, I would make some dumb-arse excuse and it would be over – but this girl, oh shit, she grabbed me, hook, line and sinker.

I was at my mate's daughter's birthday party back in Skelmersdale and my friend came over and said, "Hey, Paul, our Terri thinks that you're fit. She won't come over here. You should go and talk to her. Don't tell her I said anything."

Fuck me. I was smitten instantly. She was taller than me, beautiful eyes, gorgeous hair, tall, slim body. Shit she could have asked me for my bank card and pin number and I would have given it to her on the spot.

We quickly consumed one another in every way. She came over to Holland to see me. I felt like a movie star. When she walked through Arrivals, every fella in that airport seemed to be looking at her and she was with me. Hook, line and sinker is an understatement. Have a guess what happened? I fucked that up as well.

We lasted three months. This, for me, was a record. I went and got myself involved in a gangsters' beef back in England that had direct consequences for someone close to her. Fuck it, I am a prick. She left me and I went back to Italy to nurse my wounds.

While I was sat on the beach in Pietra Ligure, I had what felt like half a house brick stuck in my chest. I had never felt that before. The relationships that I'd ruined in the past hadn't hurt like this – the pain from those would come back to haunt me much later. But now, the loss of love hit me hard. I made my mind up that I would not fall for another girl, not fuckin ever.

I spent the rest of the year going out with a variety of girls, nothing serious, just dating.

My mate's girlfriend asked me one night, "Why don't you find a nice girl and settle down?"

I just laughed and said, "I always find nice girls. I either can't, or don't want to hold on to them."

I could see her mind doing overtime, but I didn't think much more about it.

I went out with a gang of Den Haag football fans on New Year's Eve. I got really drunk and woke up on New Year's Day 2008 with a terrible hangover. My mate called me and asked me to come to Ton's Café in Rijswijk near to The Hague. We arranged to meet at three. I really couldn't be bothered going but I made the effort.

Little did I know that it was a blind date. This gorgeous little black girl is sitting at the bar with my mate and his girlfriend. When I sat down, my friends got up and moved to another table, leaving me and this little hottie to get on with it. Like I said, I had no idea that it was a blind date so I just made her laugh and told her a few wild tales. We said our goodbyes and I promised her that the next time we met I would make her pancakes with Nutella.

I didn't have to wait long. The following day she called me and asked if I wanted to go out with her. I couldn't believe it, she was lovely but I didn't think that she would ring me. I really didn't have a clue what my mates were up to.

Things happened so fast, and within three months we were living together at my place. By the end of summer 2008 we had a new house. I hadn't wanted another relationship after Terri – I was determined not to – but that idea lasted all of five minutes. Maybe it's my addictive personality but within days of meeting my blind date, I was besotted.

For the next year or so, we got on so well. We had our little house in a quiet street next to the park. Life could not have been better, and then the markets crashed around the world and the so-called 'crisis' hit Holland.

The work began to dry up. I held on for as long as I could, but I had to let a lot of guys go. I was down to just myself and four lads on site.

Thankfully since 2007, I had been paying into what is known in Holland as Zwart Bow. Translated it means, 'black building'. This is where you pay into a fund run by a group of investors. They build flats, factories, whatever, not paying any duty on anything. They fiddle with the paperwork, sell off everything and then all the investors get a share of the total return. The money is moved around by what is known as Hawala Banking.

Let's say that one guy will be in Holland, and he wants to move €100,000 to the UK. He's not going to run the risk of carrying it across the borders – he takes his money to whoever is running the Hawala system in Holland.

He pays three per cent commission on the total amount, and then a phone call is made to the UK where another guy will be running the Hawala system over there, letting him know that someone will be coming to collect the €100,000 and how he will be identified.

The guy who wants the money transferred is given a bank note, just a five or ten euro note. The serial number is sent to the handler in the UK. When the guy arrives in the UK, he hands over the bank note and is reunited with his money. Simple.

My Geordie mate got me on to it by telling me it was a

sure thing and for a while he was right. From 2007 to 2009, we kept putting money into this scheme, always getting a good return. You could take your money out at any time, with a bit of notice, of course, or you could leave it where it was and your investment would just keep growing.

Over the two years we both had paid in over €100,000 each, and now with the crisis hitting hard we decided to cash in and walk away.

My Geordie mate had called them in January 2010, and it was almost five months later when the call came to go and collect our money.

On the Monday, my mate asked me if I would drive to Breda with him to pick the money up on the Thursday. I said I would go with him. On the Wednesday morning, my phone rings and it's him again, telling me that the money had to be picked up that morning. Straight away I didn't like the sound of it.

"Look mate all you have to do is go and meet him at Amstelveen Train Station," he said.

I said to him, "If it's so simple, you go and get it."

"Paul I would if I could but I am on site in Groningen. He is there now, so just jump into a taxi and go and get it, or we will have to wait weeks until he's back up from Belgium."

Reluctantly I called a taxi, but I didn't like what was happening. I knew that something was wrong. A text message came through. My mate had given this stranger my number. I was fuckin furious. I called my mate and I had a ten-minute raging argument with him in front of the taxi driver. I called the delivery guy when I was two minutes from the train station. He had the cheek to complain about having to wait around. I reminded this gabby twat that he was a fuckin day early.

I noticed a police car parked in the forecourt of the petrol station which spooked me a little, but by now I was angry so I thought *Fuck it, I am here now*. I got out the taxi and this guy is waving to me from the Euro Lines office. I walked over to him, and he doesn't ask for the bank note, he just makes his way to a silver BMW parked across the road. He opens the boot and I put the bag of money inside my sports bag and I walk off.

He follows me across the road and asks me, "You must be making a lot of money off the drugs that you're taking to England."

"What the fuck are you going on about? I don't have anything to do with drugs." I barked at him.

"Well, where do you get all this money from?" he asked.

I'm wound up now.

"Lad get in your car and fuck off; I'm getting a taxi."

As I walked across the road, I noticed a little bald guy at the bus stop, sitting up straight with his hands in his pockets. If this was drug money or anything to do with drugs, I would never have gone to Amstelveen Train Station, not in a million years.

I walked into the station to get a bottle of water and a sandwich. When I came out of the shop, I was jumped on and thrown to the floor, and the bag was dragged out of my hand.

"Do you have weapons? Do you have weapons?" Came the voice now standing over me.

I looked up, and there was the little bald guy from the bus stop, pointing his gun right in my face, the other cops now pinning me to the ground. My hands handcuffed, I was dragged out of the station and thrown in the back of a van. When I got to the police station, the worst thing I did was to listen to the solicitor.

"My advice to you Mr McCarthy is to say 'No comment' during the interview."

So that's what I did. "No comment. No comment. No comment."

It was the worst advice that anyone could have given me, because now, the Dutch coppers are convinced that I am an English drug trafficker, caught red-handed with his ill-gotten gains.

I got two years for money laundering. A Pakistani guy and a Moroccan were in court the same time as me. The prosecution tried to put us all together. I couldn't believe what was happening. Once they had established that we were not connected, the Moroccan guy who was caught with a handgun gets bail. The Pakistani fella who was caught with over a million euros in his house, and notebooks logging all his transactions, gets bail. There is no mention of bail in my case; I got two years that fuckin afternoon.

My solicitor came down to the cells to see me. I was fuming.

"Two fuckin years! Are you fuckin stupid?"

"Don't worry Mr McCarthy we can appeal; this seems very excessive."

One of the worst things about going to prison this time was that I was managing a band from Skelmersdale called The Endeavours. They were a great band. They had a few teething problems with one another, but they worked well together. I had got them into a studio in Ashton near Manchester and we'd produced an EP. I paid my son and his production team to come and document everything. They made several music videos and I travelled with them to film their gig in Hyde Park. The band went on to win MTV's Newcomer and, while I was in prison here in Holland, they were all flown to the Seychelles where they played to over 10,000 people.

I had paid for everything, and I missed out on most of it. They broke up not long after. Gutted again.

I ended up doing seven months in Rotterdam Prison until the appeal was granted. I was released pending the appeal. My intention now was to tell the court what the money was for, and to explain that I had taken €100,000 from my account to pay it back to the tax office because that's where it really belonged. I also wanted to explain that the advice I was given by my solicitor was a load of bollox.

I was released from prison on 10 November 2010. I had to wait to be informed of the appeal date.

I went back home with my tail between my legs. My missus was waiting for me with enough hugs and kisses to kill a teddy bear. They took €384,440 off me when I was arrested. They even took the €800 that I had in my wallet. I never saw a penny of it. Wounded again.

I went back to work in no time, but the work was drying up quickly. It was harder and harder to get paid by the companies who I worked for. I was still owed money from a firm in Rotterdam for work that I had carried out back in 2008. A firm from Eindhoven owed me €16,500 going back to 2007. Every excuse under the sun was given.

I phoned the firm in Rotterdam and I said to the Director, "Just admit that you've got no money and I will see you when you do have money, just be straight with me."

He was too proud to admit that he was clinging on by his balls. It cost me €3,000 through a solicitor to get back €12,000, and things were becoming desperate.

I was sick of the false promises. Money was running out all over Holland and companies were going under left, right and centre. I began thinking about getting back to work trafficking drugs. I was good at it, so I thought: *Just until this bad patch blows over. I could move a bit of stuff just to keep me afloat.*

Thankfully I got a permanent contract with a company out of De Lier, in the south of Holland. My drug-trafficking idea was put aside, at least for now.

The year 2011 to 2012 was the worst that I had had in a long time. My father died in March 2011, which absolutely destroyed me. My heart and my soul were broken in two.

In August 2011, my girlfriend and I had our first child. I was so happy but, inside, I was a broken man. I couldn't get over my father's death. The day that he died, my mother was taken into a home suffering with dementia. My family life in the UK was over in a second, and for the first time in my life, I felt like I was homeless, really homeless.

I started drinking again, only this time I was hammering it. I would wake up in the back of my work van covered in my own piss. I would then go straight to work, and the cycle would continue. My girl left me and moved in with her mother. With her and the baby gone, I thought that was it – my selfish, addictive nature had taken hold again.

Before long I was sniffing coke and smoking crack. This time I really did want to self-destruct to the point of death.

I had had enough.

In my mind I had given up completely. I slept in my work van more than I slept at home. The house was empty without my girl and my kid. I couldn't even face going home. I would go to the first pub that I could find, drink and sniff coke until they threw me out at God knows what time. I would fall asleep in the back of the van, night after night. This went on, and my mate said that I could stay at his place until I sorted myself out.

One day I was sitting watching the news and they re-ran the story of Amy Winehouse's death. I was too consumed by my own grief to really pay attention when she died back in July 2011. Now watching this on TV, it really upset me – that tiny little thing, being carried out on that trolley. I sat there almost crying as I watched her go from greatness to her death, my hands shaking as I fought back the tears.

That trolley scene just kept on playing in my mind. Every time that I had a drink or I sniffed a line, I would see that fuckin trolley. I began to realise that if I continued with what I was doing, I would end up on a trolley just like Amy.

This sounds awful but watching Amy's death being broadcast again like this, it woke me up.

Different triggers over the years have either sent me down a rocky road or they have brought me back from the brink. This pattern of behaviour has gone on throughout my life.

The sadness and the tragedy of her death made me realise that what I was doing was wrong and that I had so much to live for. I was determined to get my girl and my kid back again. I started training and I stopped using drugs. I was still drinking but nowhere near as much as before.

By the end of 2012, my family was back together again. We had a new apartment, brand new. I bought all new furniture. The last place where I had lived, I sold everything to the girl upstairs for €1,000. I gave her the keys for the apartment and told her to lock the door behind her and put the keys through the letter box when she had finished taking everything. I drove away never to return.

Throughout my life I had walked away like this. As soon as a relationship got shitty or I felt that I was becoming too involved, I would just split, as easy as that. Most of the people who I had left behind would haunt me years later because, after each failed relationship, I would dwell on the old ones wondering what might have been.

I had filled another girl's house with new furniture once. I had only been with her a couple of months. She pissed me off so I left, just taking my passport and a pair of new trainers. I left all my belongings behind because everything would have reminded me of her

Now, having a new place with my girl and my kid I had it decorated real nice. I was now back on track and nothing was going to bring me down again.

I had told my girl about what went on with Radiohead over many months. She kept on at me to do something about it, so I wrote a 70-page statement and sent it to Davenport Lyons, a law firm in London. One of their solicitors contacted me and, after reading the statement, he told me that he was thinking about contacting Radiohead's lawyers to see what they had to say about it, but first he wanted to discuss it with his partners.

At the end of 2012, I met a guy who offered to give me ten kilos of heroin at the price he was paying for it, all I had to do was get it to England, sell it and we would split the profit between us. Like a dickhead, I told him that I would think about it. Up until February 2013 he kept on at me, making the offer more and more desirable. The price in Holland for one kilo of heroin at the time was €19,000. If I got it to England, I could sell it for £34,000.

I decided to take him up on his offer – don't ask me why. I thought that it would be an easy few quid.

I got to the border at Calais. The customs officers were waiting for me. They took me straight to the shed and went right for the stash. They knew exactly where to look. Apart from me, there were only two other people in the whole world who knew where the heroin was hidden.

The customs officers jacked up my truck. The three of them lay on the floor shining their torches. This is how the conversation went:

"How do we get into it?"

"See them two straps there?"

"Yes."

"You take them off, drop that bit down. It's in there."

"Where?"

He then pointed and said wildly, "IN THERE!"

I knew that I was fucked as soon as I saw the trolley jacks when I drove into the shed.

One of the guys who knew where the heroin was stashed has never been in touch, despite the fact that he owes me €26,000. He was one of my closest friends for over ten years.

He knows where I have been for the past five and a half years and he has never asked about me, or phoned my missus to offer any financial assistance. You don't have to be a rocket scientist to work this one out.

What you will soon come to understand when working with these kinds of people is that you are only wanted when you're lining their pockets.

You go from, "He's sound him, lad – fuckin fearless – he's got balls of steel", "Top grafter, he is; he can get you anything," to being called a "fuckin liability".

One thing goes wrong and you're a liability. They're quick to forget all the money that you've earned for them over the years. It's also a way for them to distance themselves from you, of course. They scarper like the fuckin rats they are. Most of them live in fear of going to prison because they haven't got the balls to do the job. I once did, and I am telling you now, trafficking drugs is a drug in itself.

Getting your product across borders and beating the customs officers is more exhilarating than any chemical that I've ever taken. Every time I went through customs – no matter what or how much I was carrying – the prolonged rush that I felt would last until I hit the motorway.

It's such an amazing feeling when you drive out of the customs bay. It's as if someone has been pulling your head backwards slightly, like they're holding onto a rope that's attached to the back of your head. It starts just as you get to whichever border you are about to cross. It stays there, no matter how long you are kept in the customs bay while they ransack your vehicle. When they don't find it and they give you your keys back, the rush doesn't stop there. I would drive out of the customs bay unable to smile or show any emotion but inside I would be buzzing like fuck.

"Almost there, almost there." I would keep saying to myself.

Once back on the motorway, the feeling of this rope attached to the back of your head gets a little less tense. The further away from the border you get, the realisation sets in that you have made it. It's as if someone is releasing the rope bit by bit until finally you begin to relax. I would keep my teeth clenched tight and scream with excitement, still not showing any emotion on my face just in case anyone was watching.

This whole experience could last for hours. No drug I have ever taken could compare to it, for me it was just another addiction.

Two Liverpool gangsters sent money every month to my missus and to my kid for a while. They had to leave Liverpool not long after, so the money stopped. Another lad who I had worked with went around telling everyone that he was the one giving my missus the money. He never gave her a fuckin carrot. Even now he swears that the money was from him.

He phoned my missus about eight times and said that he was on his way with some money, telling her not to go out until he got there. Never once did he show up. My other mate told me that he sits in the boozer back home, lying to people about how he's given me thousands over the years, and that he's the one who kept the roof over my bird's head. Fuckin prick, I hope that he and his friends get to read this because they will know who I am on about. Gangster, my arse.

Well anyway, back to that shed in Calais. The customs officers got the drugs out and I was arrested. They handcuffed me and put me in the back of a Renault Scenic. Two hours later, I was handcuffed to the wall in Priory Court, the NCA's headquarters in Dover. They tried questioning me. They got the usual two fingers and go-and-fuck-yourself attitude right from the start.

I had already resigned myself to the fact that I would not be going home for a long time. I had left my missus and my kid behind, and that's all that I could think about. I didn't give a shit about myself or the fact that I had lost the drugs.

My truck was confiscated. I didn't give a shit about that either. Just the thought of not seeing my family was chewing a hole in the side of my head, so these customs officers could go and fuck themselves for all I cared.

I was taken to Canterbury Police Station and charged with importation, Category 1. I was remanded into custody and sent to HMP Elmley on the Isle of Sheppey, just off the coast of Kent.

Once I had got over the initial shock, I called the solicitor at Davenport Lyons and explained where I was. He then told me that, due to my circumstances, he would not be able to represent me at this time, especially while I was facing the charge of importation. I was gutted, even so I understood his decision and I respected it.

I didn't call him again, my parting words were, "I'll call you when I'm free."

He laughed a little and wished me good luck.

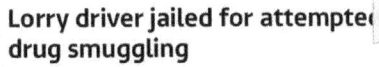

> **Lorry driver jailed for attempted drug smuggling**
>
> *Packages seized after lorry driver tried to smuggle them into the UK Credit: Border Force*
>
> A British lorry driver was been jailed for 10 years after attempting to smuggle heroin through the Channel Tunnel at Dover.
>
> Border Force officials seized around nine kilos of heroin which have an estimated street value of up to £690,000.
>
> Canterbury Crown Court heard that officers at the Channel Tunnel entrance in France stopped a Dutch-registered transit van being driven by Paul McCarthy on March 11, 2013.

This is my biggest mistake ever. Now I'm off to jail for a very long time. I fucked up big time – but you know what? I'm a much better person now. Prison really did save me – and I don't care what you hardcore wannabe gangsters have to say about what happened. You're all full of shit. I met more honest criminals in prison than you lot put together.

I spent the next nine months just getting on with things, quickly following a routine. This is the first time that I came across a drug called 'spice'. It is the most disgusting drug anyone could have the misfortune of becoming addicted to.

I swear, many times, the guards have said to me, "I wish that we could turn a blind eye to people smoking hash because this spice shit is fucking deplorable."

Spice, sometimes called 'fish' is a chemical compound used for transporting coy carp. If you move coy carp they can become very distressed and die, so this chemical is fed to them to calm them down. Some twisted fuck decided to smoke it one day, and before you know it, it was a prison epidemic. It's highly addictive, much more than heroin and crack combined.

Spice is a physical and a mental addiction rolled into one. I met lads in prison who told me that they were hardcore heroin users and were now smoking spice. They had given up on the heroin. Spice is so cheap to make. You order the chemicals online and then you buy a sack of dried banana leaves or some other cheap dried product, spray it with the chemical cocktail and get some poor sod to keep smoking it until it's strong enough. You get roughly two grams for ten quid. Heroin in prison, you get about 0.2 of a gram for 10 quid. The heroin addicts were prime targets for the spice dealers.

I saw so many good lads fall by the wayside due to spice. It's fucking disgusting. The prison officers are in a constant battle trying to keep this shit out of prison, but the dealers are smart. They would have their children draw or paint them pictures, then they would get their mates to spray these pictures with the chemicals. They would dry the picture out and then send it as if it was a gift to Daddy. The junkies would then buy a strip of coloured paper, about the size of a couple of match sticks, for five pounds.

Spice became stronger and stronger as the dealers learnt through the internet how to mix their chemicals. One strain was given the name Mamba, after the snake, because it was so strong it could kill you. The poor lifeless junkies would smoke it and then they would collapse in a puddle of their own puke. I saw several of them pissing and shitting themselves while convulsing on the floor.

There was so much of the stuff in prison, that the dealers would give the junkies a massive packed joint and tell them that they could have it for free if they smoked half of it straight away. They call this 'the spice challenge'. It's awful to see but the dealers and the lads standing around get a kick out of watching these poor cunts almost die in front of them. The paramedics would be called every time.

One of the most disturbing things that I saw was in HMP Hindley Prison in Wigan. A young lad addicted to spice was standing at the top of the stairs pleading with one of the dealers for a joint. Even though he had no money, the dealer was standing on the top step with the junkie a couple of steps below him. The dealer shouts to all the young lads on the top floor to go and get their phones. At least ten lads came back with iPhones and Galaxys. The dealer gets them all to start recording. He then opens his dressing gown, showing his now naked body. The junkie kneels down in front of him, cups his balls in one hand and wanks him with the other while pleading for a joint. All the young lads were laughing and shouting abuse at the junkie. I started shouting at the dealer. I felt so sorry for this kid. He is now all over the internet, degraded for the whole world to see.

I pleaded guilty at Canterbury Crown Court and within minutes the judge gave me twelve years. No basis for a plea. She then took two years off for my early plea of guilty. I was now on my way to HMP Swaleside, the big house. I had heard so much about this place while I was on remand and not much of it was good.

When I arrived at Swaleside I have to be honest, my arse fell out. When I got to my cell in D wing and the door shut behind me, I had my first-ever panic attack. I thought I was going to drop dead on the spot, then a voice came across the landing.

"Paul, is that you? Paul? It's me, Wes."

Thank the fuck, I thought.

I had made friends with a lad from Liverpool while I was on remand, and now here he is across the landing. I calmed down straight away. We arranged to see one another the next day.

It didn't take long to settle in at Swaleside. The screws (prison officers) there had been in the game for years, so they knew exactly how to deal with the inmates. Once again, I quickly got into a routine, going to class to get re-educated.

I couldn't spell the simplest of words. I am dyslexic, but the way that I was when I started in class was sad to say the least. I couldn't read properly until I addressed my dyslexia. I would use words in a sentence that shouldn't be there, like 'phew' and 'few'. I was embarrassed when I was turning in papers to the teacher – 45 years old and embarrassed like a child. I had to do something about it.

I signed in at the library and the first book that I took out was the Oxford Dictionary. I tried to memorise a page a night. The dyslexia makes it so difficult to remember things. I would read the page over and over again. When hearing a word on the TV that I was unsure about, I would reach for the dictionary and try to memorise that word. Eventually my vocabulary grew to the point where I became more and more confident and coherent in conversation.

I had now been in prison for over a year, drug-free and using every second that I had to better myself. I know that my qualifications are nothing compared to most people, but for me, it's fantastic. All the teachers who I came across were so kind and they went out of their way to help me achieve. I started reading with the aid of a blue screen. Normally I would give up on a book after about three or four pages, now I could finish a book in a week.

As I had knuckled down and I wasn't in any trouble, I was given a job at the DHL warehouse. Thirty-six quid a week. I was moved to a much better wing with a bit more freedom. I made friends quickly. Some of these guys were doing life. The average sentence was ten years-plus. I had one of the shortest sentences, so I didn't talk about it at all. It's not right to mention that you have two years left or say things like, "I can't wait to go home," because most of these lads were never getting out.

One lad who lived downstairs from me was selling his Terada Spanish guitar. He sold it to me for a packet of Golden Virginia Tobacco.

I once again became obsessed. I had only played on and off over the past 20 years so I had to teach myself all over again. Funny how things come back to you.

The songs – and the events that inspired them – came back to me, too. When I was about 11 years old, I was robbed for my sweets a couple of times on the way home from school. I would come out of the shop, and two lads from West Bank High School would grab me and empty my pockets. I told my mate Gary Cahill about these two. Gary was tough as fuck – no one messed with him. He was a year older than me, even so we have been friends for life.

Gary says to me, "I'll walk home with you today and see if they get you again."

I asked him to ask Anthony Hartford to go with us, as I had already paid Anthony £1.86 to beat up another kid called Frank.

Gary didn't need anyone, he just said, "Leave that to me."

I went into the shop to get my sweets and when I came

out Gary was gone. I was on my way home and sure enough the two lads were waiting for me. They were much bigger than me. One of them grabbed me and pushed me against the fence while the other kid tried getting his hand inside my pocket. The next thing, the lad with his hand in my pocket gets punched in the face. Gary then does a 360 and smacks the other lad in the mouth. The two bullies pick up their school bags and they scarper like fuck, never to be seen again. As they were running away, I took out my bag of sweets and I shared them with Gary.

I shouted after them, "You're not so fuckin tough now, are yer?"

Gary ruffled my hair and he started laughing; we talked about that 360 punch for years.

This event gave me the inspiration to compose a song called *Infamy*. I started writing it back in 1982. It was a play on words:

> *In for me, you've got it in for me*
> *Don't you walk down my street*
> *I'm gonna knock you off your feet*
> *You better pray that we never meet*
> *I'll do my best to knock out your teeth*

Now sitting in my cell, I re-wrote that song – and many more from my childhood. The officer on the wing suggested that I put in for a transfer to HMP The Mount in Hertfordshire as soon as I got my Category C status.

I asked him, "Why the Mount?"

"You'll love it there. They have a music class and a recording booth."

I thought that he was taking the piss out of me. The next thing, he had printed out the details from the Mount's website and, sure enough, they ran a City and Guilds course in Sound Engineering and Music Technology. I couldn't wait to get my Category C status.

Going back to my time at The Lamb Inn, I was given a roebuck, a small deer-like animal. It had been hit by a car. One of the farmers had brought it to the kitchen to see if I wanted to butcher it. I wouldn't touch it, so he threw it in the woods behind the restaurant.

After a few weeks, I went and cut its head off, by now the skull had had all the flesh eaten off it by maggots. I left it hanging for a few more days. Thom asked me what I was going to do with it. I told him that I planned to boil it until it was bleached white, then sit it on top of my TV.

It took a lot of work to get the last few maggots out from inside the brain cavity. Once it was completely clean, I dried it out in the oven on a low heat. When it was finished, it looked cool as fuck – a bleached-white skull with two short stubbed horns. It really did resemble something from a horror film, like the skull of a demon.

I was sitting at healthcare in Swaleside one afternoon and

on the table in the waiting room was a copy of Q Magazine. I glanced over it and I noticed that there was a feature about Radiohead. I flicked through the pages and the first thing that I saw was Thom's photo. The band were somewhere in America. They were all in a junk shop. Jonny is looking at the old cameras, and Thom is sitting next to a bleached-white skull with massive horns, I think it was from a bull. Thom has a look of defiance on his face – was that for my benefit?

Like I said before, all the little things may not appear to have any significance on their own, but when you put them into context and see them as I do, I hope that you can appreciate how fucking freaked out I have been over the years. Everything that I have seen or heard has played on my mind in one way or another. Believe me, I have questioned my sanity on many occasions.

I couldn't wait to get out of Swaleside. One morning I was standing outside DHL talking with a Pakistani kid. He was about twenty-six. We were waiting to go into work. Everyone was outside in the morning sunshine, smoking and chatting.

A young black guy walks up to the lad who I am talking to and asks, "Did you ring my sister last night?"

The Pakistani kid replies with, "No, I didn't. What you on about you fucking dickhead?"

The black kid swiped him across the face. I thought he had tried to punch him. He then says, "Who's the dickhead now?"

The Pakistani kid puts his hand on the left side of his face and, as he pulls it away to see if there's any blood, the cheek falls open and I could see his teeth through the side of his face. The black kid has slashed him with a razor blade. My stomach turned. I think that I went the colour of boiled shite.

That was the thing about Swaleside. If something happened it was generally fucking horrible. I wanted to leave after that, not because I was scared, but because I had been there long enough. It was definitely time to move on.

I arrived at HMP The Mount in Hemel Hempstead, Hertfordshire, and the first question that I asked was where the music department was. I couldn't wait to get started. I had to go through the induction period of about a week. I applied for a job at DHL and, because of my time at DHL Swaleside I was hired straight away.

I had to wait four weeks until the next music programme started as they ran every eight weeks. The course was that City and Guilds in Sound Engineering and Music Technology that I told you about before.

Ian, the music teacher, went through the recording process and straight away he booked me in to record my first track. I have to be honest, I was a fish out of water. I was so nervous my gut was aching. Ian, being the great teacher that he is, reassured me that everyone has to start somewhere.

"Just relax, Paul. Your song is great, and your guitar sound is really good."

At first I recorded the guitars working to a click. It's so fucking annoying, so Ian suggested having a basic drum beat on the computer and then playing it through my headphones, just so that I could get my timing right. There was a young lad in the studio who sung backing vocals on my track. I couldn't believe after all these years that I was finally doing it.

I couldn't be kept out of the studio. Even on my days off I tried to get back in there. I passed my exams and I received my certificates. Along with the certificates came an offer to collaborate with an outside charity called Finding Rhythms. The idea was to work together as a team to achieve a B-tech in Sound Engineering – an extra course that would allow us to produce an LP. The record would then be sold online to raise money to help young offenders create their own music in the future.

The charity came to the prison once a week. We would have four hours a day over the next twelve weeks to write and produce our own song for the album. There was no pressure. I went through my 25-year-old back catalogue and chose one of my oldest tracks, *Take Me Back*. My voice is not the best, so I asked one of the young women who worked with us to rehearse the song. We performed the track and it was greeted with a rapturous round of applause. I was in my element.

It was back in 1982 when I first longed for the adoration of an audience. Katrina's younger sister, Lorraine, asked me to dance with her in front of the hundred or so kids who attended the Green Hill Disco, some kind of strange jazz ballet that she had been working on. The dance routine was set to *Bohemian Rhapsody* by Queen. The DJ introduces the both of us. Lorraine glides onto the dance floor wearing a floral gown with flowing tails and cuffs, her long brown hair flowing down her back.

She beckons me to join her and I freeze. I've lost my bottle. Lorraine blows me a kiss and she dances her heart out. She was absolutely amazing and when she finished her routine, the whole place erupted into mass hysteria. Everyone was wildly applauding her, whistles and cheers rang out. She came and sat next to me, and she asked me why I didn't dance with her. I told her that I didn't want to ruin her performance, but the truth was I was chicken. The applause that Lorraine had received was what I had longed for. I wanted it so, so badly.

Back in HMP The Mount, after receiving my first-ever round of applause, my focus was on writing songs and then performing them for the lads in the wing. They were a tough audience. I have not taken any drugs in prison. I have never even smoked a joint. I have never even played a game of pool because that would have meant that I am truly a prisoner, in my mind at least. The young lads would sit there stoned out of their nuts while I played a selection of my tunes for them.

There was always one doughnut who would shout across the landing, "Can you play Wonderwall?"

My old mate Eric Parker told me, on many occasions, never to copy anyone. This is how he explained the best piece of advice that I've ever been given about music:

"Look Paul, anyone can play someone else's songs – that's easy – but writing your own shows people truly what you're all about. Picasso never painted any of Rembrandt's paintings, so why should you sing other people's songs? Stick to your guns, lad, and do your own thing."

I never play anyone else's songs, never; I think it's a fuckin cop out.

One of the young lads on my wing told me that he was an R&B singer, so I asked him to come into the studio to have a look around. Little did he know that my intention was to have him record the backing vocals on a track that I was working on.

Maleek was well-known throughout the prison system and once we had recorded this track, he was hooked – he was in and out of the studio just as much as I was. Working with Maleek gave me a bit of credibility with the young lads who fancied themselves as artists. From then on, I was making beats for the young rappers, playing guitar on several tracks. I also produced a track, creating all the music for a rapper called Jimmy Brima. Everyone respected Jimmy, he was well-known as a London gangster.

I was standing in line, waiting to go into healthcare one day and two lads started rapping Jimmy's track, "Busting Duke's in the trap house, Busting Duke's in the trap house."

I am standing there listening with a grin on my face. They had no idea that I had worked on the song for Jimmy. I was buzzing my head off. I quickly got a name for myself but this time in a good way.

People would refer to me like this: "You know that Scouse fella, the white lad who's always in the studio? You know, the one who's always playing his guitar?"

Doesn't sound like much really, I know, but then I think back to when people referred to me like this: "You know that Scouse lad who is always out of his nut selling drugs?"

My mum died around this time. She had suffered with dementia for a few years. I don't think she ever got over the fact that my dad was gone. The Imam came to see me, and he allowed me to use the phone to call my brother. Andy has dealt with prisoners for over thirty years, he has worked for the Prison Service since he left the army. He explained that, although she was gone, at least she was with my dad and the nightmare that is dementia was at last over for her.

This really helped me to accept Mum's passing. It's absolutely fucked up being locked in your cell with no one to turn to. Dealing with grief behind a door has a terrible effect on you. I had to vent my anger and for some reason I chose to target Andy. I sent him a couple of fucked-up letters. I was having an emotional meltdown. The only way to deal with it was by transferring my anger onto him. I didn't plan it, it just happened.

Security refused to let me go to Mum's funeral. The Imam again came to my rescue. He went to see The Governor on my behalf. After that I got permission to attend with three officers from my wing escorting me from Hemel Hempstead up to St Helens in Merseyside. I was only allowed to go to the crematorium. The officers and their driver sat in the minibus with me handcuffed in the back.

My mates started to arrive, black Mercedes, black Audis, black BMWs. My friend Tommy turns up in a black Mondeo with all the chrome work and blacked-out windows. As soon as they saw me in the back of the minibus, they all came walking over.

Mr Manning, who was escorting me, turned to me and asks, "Are we going to be all right here Mac?"

"Don't worry," I said. "No one's going to do anything at my mother's funeral."

The minibus was soon surrounded, and I could see that the officers were getting more and more agitated. Mr Manning pushes on the automatic lock and seals us in. The lads start talking to me through a gap in the window. I then tell Mr Manning that my brother Andy has just arrived. Mr Manning was already aware that our Andy worked for the Prison Service. He relaxed and took the lock off the door. I was allowed to stand outside but I was handcuffed to another officer, Mr O, who was about six foot seven, a big tough-looking black guy.

While we were talking, one of my old school friends drives in with his wife, parks his black Mercedes right in front of us. Anthony Hartford was the lad who I told you about before, the lad who I paid at school to beat up Frank.

Anthony just stands there, staring over not saying a word. I had seen that look on his face many times before and it never ended well for whoever was on the receiving end. I made eye contact and he came walking over. Everyone moved out the way as if it was the parting of the waves. Anthony still has this look on his face. I could feel Mr O's hand begin to shake. His adrenalin was obviously pumping.

I thought that Anthony was going to kick off, so I said to him, "Don't do anything."

"All right Paul, I won't."

Mr O, as big as he was, didn't faze Anthony at all. No one did.

We gave our mum a lovely send-off, but to this day I haven't grieved. It's impossible in prison. I almost broke down as we drove away from the crematorium but I fought it back. I didn't want the screws to see me cry.

Although I had some bad times inside, prison life has changed me for the better, in every way. It's crazy to say this, but I am so glad that I ended up in prison. I have addressed so many of my life-long issues. I have educated myself. I am articulate, fit, healthy. I have written over a hundred songs. I have a band from North Wales waiting for me to join them on my release. They listened to some of my recordings online and they got in touch to offer their services. God only knows what will happen when I get out.

My missus and my kid are waiting for me, and I fully intend to fix as many broken relationships as possible. None of my children know me, all I want to do is make them proud. Yes I am a fuck-up of the worst kind – or should I say I was.

During my life I have been in the company of many doctors and psychologists. They have all given their diagnoses. ADHD has been mentioned over the years. Last year, I requested a session with the psychologist while in prison in the UK and I was re-diagnosed as being bipolar. Since being in prison here in Holland and wanting to get myself levelled out for my release, I again had regular meetings with the mental health team. I was sent to see a psychiatrist and, after a couple of months, I was re-diagnosed as borderline bipolar and cluster B. I think this means that I am 'double nutty'.

Over the past few months, I have been trying a different medication. We have all decided that 100 milligrams of quetiapine a day is working best. My emotions are a lot more controlled, and I am having a lot less hyperactive episodes. It's as if I have put on a hat and it's keeping me calm and controlled.

After talking with the mental health team for so long, I finally understand why everything in my life has been so black and white, so troubled. The decisions that I had made when walking away from people and places. Leaving my comfortable surroundings in search of self-destruction when something went wrong, instead of trying to fix it. My ability to change from friend to foe in an instant.

At first this all sounded to me like a cop-out – an excuse for my destructive behaviour. It's only after being given the opportunity to really look and listen to yourself that you realise that a donkey doesn't know that he's a donkey, just like I didn't think for one minute that there was anything wrong with me.

Assuming that you are a fuck-up when your head's not on straight is an unfair judgement of yourself. The comedian Ruby Wax's approach to her mental health issues really helped me to focus on myself. I would like to thank her and all the health workers who I have come across while in prison. Each and every one of them has helped me in one way or another.

I summed it all up when talking with the psychiatrist. She asked me, "So, Paul, can you describe how the medication is making you feel?"

And with one word, I replied, "Determined."

I have ended up back in a Dutch jail due to my own actions. While I was in prison in the UK, I made several attempts through Immigration and the Cross Border Team to be sent back to Holland so that I could be close to my missus and my kid.

They continually refused, each of them giving the same reason, "Mr McCarthy, you are a British citizen. You have no right to go and serve your sentence in Holland."

I provided more than enough evidence to show that I had lived in Holland for over ten years. I also provided them with enough evidence to prove my family ties.

After numerous attempts to get someone to listen to me, their final refusal came like this, "Mr McCarthy you do realise that immigration in Holland can refuse your return due to the crime that you have committed?"

I was bullied into silence. I couldn't believe the level that they would stoop to because they couldn't be arsed to fill in a PSI 52/2011 request on my behalf. Article 8 of the European Convention of Human Rights says that I have the right to a private and to a family life and that no public authority can interfere with this right. The convention rights of a child give my son more rights than I do to have his father close to him. My rights were not observed because, as they put it, I was a British citizen.

Discriminated against by my own country – what kind of bullshit is that? I submitted my own PSI 52/2011 request along with a Polish lad who was two cells away from me. We both sent our applications on the 21 September 2013. He had a girlfriend and two kids in Holland living in Utrecht. I had a girlfriend and one child living in The Hague. The Polish guy and I were both in prison for importing heroin into the United Kingdom.

In December 2013, he was taken to HMP Wandsworth Prison to await removal back to Holland. I was sure that I would be next.

Three months went by, I wrote a letter to Christopher Bins office at the Cross Border Team complaining that I had had no response. The letter of refusal that I received back was not signed by anyone. It was just printed at the bottom, "*Yours sincerely, The Cross Border Team*".

I had to come up with another plan. I tried for the next year and a half to get someone to help me. My probation officer also refused, telling me that, as I was in possession of a British passport, I was not entitled to serve my sentence in Holland. I resigned myself to the fact that I would have to sit out my time in the United Kingdom.

In Christmas 2016 my missus told me that the cops had been to the house to remind me that I had lost my appeal for the money-laundering charge back in 2010. The appeal only got to court in 2012; I was in the United Kingdom from 2012 onwards, so I had no idea what the outcome of the appeal was. The police in The Hague had a warrant for me but it wasn't a warrant of arrest. It was issued so that I could arrange with the court to come back to prison in Holland and finish my last five months there.

I contacted the police officer who had been to my house and asked him if he could make the warrant into a European arrest warrant – that way I was sure that I would get back home. He said that it wasn't that kind of warrant, but he would speak to his superiors.

Three months later, I am in my cell and five security staff come bursting in. They handcuffed me, and put me in 'the block' – what we called the segregation unit.

They said, "You are going back to a B-Cat Prison because we have been informed that you have outstanding charges."

I had no idea what the fuck was going on. I was sent to HMP Preston to be processed. After a week they sent me to HMP Lancaster Farms. I still had no idea why I was being moved.

In May 2017, I was told to go to reception where I was greeted by two police officers. They handcuffed me and I was taken to Blackpool Police Station. I still had no idea why. When I arrived at the police station, I was formally arrested on a European warrant and I was told that I was on my way to HMP Wandsworth to await removal back to Holland. I was so happy that I couldn't contain myself. I started thanking everyone.

"At last, I am going home," I told them.

I was taken to Westminster Magistrates' Court the next day. When I walked into court, the judge looked at the papers, then back at me.

He then said to the prosecution, "Why have you brought

Mr McCarthy before the court so soon? He has a further fifteen months on his UK sentence. We will adjourn until 11 November."

As quick as that, it was all over. I protested at being taken over 300 miles in two days to be in court for less than three minutes. I was wasting my time. I thought, *All I am to these people is a meal ticket.*

Over the next fifteen months, I was taken four times to and from Westminster Magistrates' Court, and each time I had a different judge. I am telling you now, that they passed my case around so that they could milk the system and have their time sheets filled in.

Each court appearance would begin and end the same way. I would be collected in the morning, driven at speed directly to court in London. They would then in some cases take three months to get me back to HMP Lancaster Farms.

A journey that could be done in a few hours would see me first being dropped off at HMP Wandsworth. The transport and the prison would claim from the Government to carry and process me, and then after a few weeks I would be taken to HMP Peterborough, completely in the wrong direction, and again the Government would be charged for transporting and processing me. After one night, I would be driven to HMP Manchester, despite the fact that Lancaster Farms was only another 20 minutes up the motorway. That was too easy, after again charging for transport and for processing.

The next day I would finally be taken to Lancaster Farms.

No wonder the UK's prison system is in such a shit state. I worked out that in five years of being imprisoned in the UK, I was moved to sixteen different prisons, that is fuckin ridiculous.

Finally, my UK release date arrived, 9 March 2018. I was taken the day before to HMP Preston for what's called local release. There was no mention of the European arrest warrant. The morning of the ninth I was in reception about to be processed for the last time. My papers were on the desk. I thought, *Great, I am finally out.*

The Custodial Manager then shouts to me, "Hey Mac, there's a bus coming for you, to take you to court in London. Do you want to go?"

"Do I have to go?"

"That's up to you. We are supposed to release you today. We don't have any reason to put you on the bus. Really, it's up to you."

I asked him what would happen if I refused to go. He told me another warrant would be issued and then the cops and the National Crime Agency would be looking for a fugitive.

I thought, *fuck that*. I waited for the bus and ten days later I was back in Holland. That was the best decision that I had made in a long time.

The Paul from before would have left prison at the first instance and would go on a bender. I was obviously straight and better focused.

I sat on the plane at Heathrow Airport with the two Dutch coppers. They didn't even handcuff me. I was so happy – and believe me I was glad that I stayed in custody. This was the end and, other than the plane crashing, I was going home.

PI Zuyder Bos in Heerhugowaard, Holland, where I spent my final days as a prisoner. When I came through the blue gates to the right, I was so nervous. I walked five kilometres to the train station just to get a grip on reality. Within the first hour of being free, I noticed that I had things in my pockets for the first time in five and a half years. That freaked me out.

I am now down to my last fifteen days of prison. I can tell you, that if I ever do come back inside it will either happen because someone has fucked about with my family, or the authorities have made a mistake. I have no intention of ever coming back.

The lads in prison always say, "Never say never." I don't believe that one bit. When I say it, I mean it.

I could delve deeper and deeper into Radiohead's music and words and find more and more lyrics and reasons for this and that, but you know what? I think that I've given you enough to make up your own minds. Like I said before, I don't care if you call me a liar. Thom, the band, and I know what went on and I feel that I have given a fair and balanced account of my time with them. They can deny anything that I have said if they choose to, but I doubt very much that will happen. My solicitor told me just recently that Radiohead's lawyers would probably take out an injunction to halt the publication of my book, I do hope so. Either way, this autobiography will be available. Whether anyone buys it, only time will tell.

It really only remains for me to thank the people who have helped me through this prison sentence:

My best and most loyal friend Mr Thomas Newton from Kirkby in Merseyside – thanks Tommy for never giving up on me and always, without fail, being there to support me.

My missus and my kid, I truly don't know what I would have done without you.

Her Majesty's Prison Service and most of the people who work in prisons are truly there to help people like myself. You only ever hear the negative stories about prison life, but I can never thank them enough for the support and encouragement that I received throughout my sentence. Ian, the music teacher at HMP The Mount, is a God.

I just have to thank one more person because, without him,

this autobiography would just be a story about 'sex and drugs'.

I am so privileged to have been, at one time, friends with one of the world's greatest singers and songwriters. There is no one on this planet that can argue with that. I have no ill will towards Thom – none whatsoever – life is far too short. I am proud and thankful that he has done all that he set out to do. I did play a part in his rise to fame and fortune and, again, there's no one on this planet who can argue with that.

He has, throughout my time in prison, given me the strength to knuckle down and get on with writing this story and I have never written a song without him in mind. All my songs have been created in the hope that – if he ever gets to hear them – he would approve, even though he has no idea of the goals that I have set for myself. An autobiography about sex and drugs is fair enough, but Thom has most certainly helped to give this story its rock 'n' roll.

With that, there are really only two words left for me to say: THANKS, THOM.

One very last thing: I have wanted my name on a record for as long as I can remember, and Thom knew that from the start. I always thought that he had left me off the album *Pablo Honey*. I have explained about Thom's talent for manipulating words. Maybe I did finally get my name on a record and it was staring me in the face all the time:

Pablo Honey = Paul McCarthy.

Picture Credits

All photos taken by Paul McCarthy except where listed below:

p3 © Jaggery / The Jericho Tavern, Jericho, Oxford / CC BY-SA 2.0

p10 © Victoria Jones /Alamy

p45 © Google Images

p128 © Morning Advertiser via Google Images

p152 © Kevin Hale / Oxford old fire station / CC BY-SA 2.0

p195 © factoryfastrecords.com via Google Images

p245 © ITV Meridian via Google Images

p272 © N H Nieuws via Google Images

Milton Keynes UK
Ingram Content Group UK Ltd.
UKHW020952220724
445981UK00004B/203